Island

(the one that wasn't supposed to be)

By

Gary Wilson

Island

(the one that wasn't supposed to be)

By Gary Wilson

This book is a work of fiction. Names, characters, places and incidents are products of the author's imagination or are used fictitiously. Any resemblance to actual events or locales or persons is entirely coincidental.

Second edition

www.garywilson.ca

ISBN-13: 978-0-9784992-6-6

Acknowledgements

I wish to thank all those whose kindness and generosity have encouraged and inspired me during this undertaking, including my friends in jail and prison, Baxter, Toy (may he rest in peace), Pete, Scott, Ray, Cisco, Bamm, Carpenter, Hani, Romo, Markal, Brown, Hutto, Wymola, Dodson, Scaggs, Tap, Mayfield, Zywicki, Hall, Johnjohn, Wolverton, Zipper, Young, Cowboy, Dutch, Greywolf, Levine, Smitty, Boyd, Fennessey, Roger, Holloway, Hoover, Starkey, Henning, Jenkins, Rudy, and most of all, Maddox, Slick and Professor Silva; my friends and business colleagues, Rod, Shawn, Lloyd and Mike; my lawyers in Canada and the United States; my family in general and my parents in particular; and my wife, Julia; without each of whom this effort may never have come to fruition.

Table of Contents

Chapter 1

Truth is a subset of propaganda. Remember that, Reader.

Chapter 2

My name is, say, Barry. No, really, that is my name. Barry. Barry, uuuh, Klassen. I guess I'm a little ambiguous on this point because the driver's license in my pocket has a different name on it. I can't recall that name at this precise moment—which is bad, very foolish, very careless of me. It's always important to know your name. You never know when you may need to say it. "Hello, Officer Friendly, my name is uuuh... I mean... uuuh Barry? No, no, no, uuuh Kerry—yeah, Kerry Coddington." That, dear Reader, is not a successful verbal transaction. Officer Friendly, who otherwise is useful for directions and even, in dire circumstances (as I learned six months ago almost to the day), aid, will not respond well to such clumsiness. Happily, I can say that I have never actually fumbled quite so badly as that—though often, with so many names on God's green earth to choose from, it has only been my iron will that has kept me focused, that has kept me from dawdling too long in that name-shopper's paradise, whenever there has been a present at hand needing my full attention. (However, one time at work I did answer the phone and say, "This is Gary, I mean, Cary..." That was not adept. The coworker on the other end of the line did not matter per se, but in a spirit of discretion I very soon left that employ).

Discretion: that is the key to traveling. I like this word, "traveling." And I endorse it as descriptive of what I am doing right now (in the extended present "right now," as opposed to the ahorita kind of "right now"), what I have been doing for the last 10 months. I really do not appreciate people, like my lawyer, with their faux criminal subculture "on the lam." I do not have tattoos. I am not opportunistically eyeing every passing 7/11 for a shot at an easy $30 and change. And I do not slink through alleys looking for a fight. (Besides all that, I have yet to be arrested—so there! Case closed!) If you want to be so unnecessary with words as to say that I am traveling incognito, I could roll my eyes and say, "Sure. Fine. Alright. Whatever!" But, truth to tell, I am not even incognito. Many people have known me this past year, and known me well. The name that I received at birth is just one part of me and has proven, time and time again, to be beside the point in my interactions with others. When you go to Safeway and buy a loaf of bread, do you tell the cashier your name? Or do you care if her name "really" is Joyce, as her name-tag says, or if it "actually" is Jill? And just because her parents christened her with some verbal identifier like "Joyce," or "Jill" now, should we really be so primitive as to attach any deeper significance to the matter than simple convenience? So, in all honesty, I am simply traveling—and I am really enjoying my travels. There is nothing like a nation-wide arrest warrant hanging over your head to add a little spice to life, to keep you on your toes and teach you the existential responsibility of genuine discretion. (Whoever—my first guess would have to be that swashbuckler John Calvin—said that the life lived without intensity wasn't worth living, really hit the nail on the head.)

Chapter 3

Reader, have you ever been on the ferry that runs between Mazatlán and La Paz? I anticipate a rather uneventful passage. It is afternoon now and we will get to La Paz sometime in the morning. I doubt that I will sleep at all tonight because I am not much of an upright sleeper.

The water is so blue! I wish that scenery description was in my literary palette, because I know you would revel in the sight before my eyes. The sky is sky-blue; the sun is bright; Mazatlán, with its dry hills and mountains in the distance behind it, lies on the coast off to the right (port or starboard, seeing as how I am at sea). Every now and then we pass a strange swirl about ten or twenty feet across which I think is a school of fish of some sort, though it—or they—look(s) kind of green and sea-weedy. We also cross the tracks of fishing boats. I first noticed these boat tracks a few weeks ago when I went up the hill that the faro—the lighthouse—is on. From up there you can get a good overall view of a boat's path for many miles out to sea, and you can see far more clearly than from shore level that even after its wake is completely dissipated there is still a definite alteration to the water's surface that meanders where the boat meandered. I assume that this is pollution, a trail of oil, whether from oozing fish or oozing fuel I wouldn't know, that ever-so-slightly calms the affected serpentine for the hour or so until it too is dissipated.

The view of Mazatlán, a delightful city with delightful people and a delightful climate (and my future winter home, as I have lately determined), is best from up there, the hill of the faro. It is well worth the effort of ascent. The only bad part is getting past the sewage plant, which is at the base of the hill. The hill itself must be three hundred feet or so high. It's on what used to be an island but is now connected to the shore by a solid causeway. You can take a cab, or pulmonía, out there or, like me, ride on the bus called Playa Sur. Since sur means "south", and you're going to take the bus to the end of the line, you can see that the faro is at the southernmost tip of Mazatlán. Any further south and you have to swim the channel to La Isla de las Piedras, just a few hundred yards down the coast.

Speaking of buses, I have to tell you something funny, Reader. Public transit here in México, like everywhere, is economical. Boarding a bus is going to cost you only maybe a couple pesos, and that is roughly twenty-five cents. The price is a little different from route to route, but it is always minimal, and always posted for you on the bus. When you get on, you hand the bus-driver your payment and he in turn hands you a little receipt. You should have the exact change since the etiquette is that bus-drivers don't make change. (That is not unreasonable considering that they are on a route with a schedule (sort of) and it would be a hopeless situation if they had to divert any amount of their time to processing chicken-feed). Well, one evening a few weeks ago I got on a bus in the old part of the city and at the very next stop some tourists got on, two couples who by their conversation had just eaten at a fashionable restaurant. It was a little unusual to see people like these getting on the bus at night. Tourists use the buses frequently enough, but more in the bright sunshine of day than after dark, and these looked like taxi riders in any event. Anyway, after paying their pittance and getting their receipts, one of them asked the bus-driver for route information because they would have to make a transfer to reach their destination. Then they sat down and started fretting about transferring to the right bus. Reader, please don't ever be a tourist. Being out of your element is perfectly okay, perfectly cool, if there is a reason, a real reason. Tourism is not a real reason. People who wear Bermuda shorts and bright flower-print shirts, and who sport fresh sunburns, do not have a real reason—the world over. What makes me remember these particular tourists was a little misconception they had about their receipts, an easy mistake that I am just glad I myself never made, yet amusing to me all the same. It made them look so cheap. (And this is me, the skinflint of all skinflints talking). You've already guessed their mistake, Reader, I'm sure. They thought their receipts were transfers, of course—just as they would have been anywhere up north. However, one of them seemed to have encountered better information—though obviously not at firsthand—and brought this up uncertainly to the others, the fact that their "transfers" may have been nothing more than receipts. It was the response to this, from one in particular, that amused me so much. By goodness, he had paid his fare fair and square and nobody was going to make him pay twice. He went on and on, or at least it seemed like it. They were on the bus for only a few blocks, then they had to transfer. That two bits, four times over, really meant a lot to that guy, someone who doubtless had just spent in a day what people here live on for a month. I was tempted to transfer with them just for a laugh, but I didn't. My policy here is to evade attention and generally to avoid my fellow Nortes.

Chapter 4

Let's get something straight right now, Reader, before we go any further. I realize that you are addicted to the truth Hollywood-style. There is nothing wrong with that. I mean, it's good. You are a credit to your culture. That I have backslidden in this to some degree is a failing I strive hourly to overcome. I mean that, really! Whenever I watch an action-drama—and I discipline myself to do so daily, or at least annually—and the routine car chase results in the routine accident where the bad guy's car rear-ends a parked car and subsequently catapults high into the air (in slow motion) and twirls before crashing down, I just breathe deeply and fight the hysteria. No one's going to see my heresy! I remind myself that I have just been a witness to truth, truth Hollywood-style, and I send up a little prayer first of thanks and then of supplication for help in suppressing within myself the urge to reject—even scorn!—the enlightenment that has just been imparted to me. This is how car accidents proceed. First you hit the back end of a parked car. Then your car is launched twenty feet into the air and it makes one full pirouette before falling back to earth a hundred feet down the road. And lastly, the police pull you out of your car groggy and shaken up but unhurt enough to be shackled and hauled away. Forget any misconceptions you might have that rear-ending parked cars is just not so frequent—constant—an occurrence as all that, or that the subsequent little pirouette is just a standard, dramatic-looking action sequence that has been found to be relatively safe and simple for stuntmen to perform (the most bang for the buck); or that, instead of emerging unscathed from such mishaps, people are more likely to be left looking like bloody pretzels and needing an emergency crew with their jaws of life for mere extrication from the vehicle. Forget all that! You will never get anywhere in life believing all these little fictions and fantasies that distract you from the truth. Hollywood is the fount of all truth. That is Lesson Number One, and if you take Lesson Number One to heart then you will live long and prosper.

So, what I want to get straight with you right here and now, Reader, is the fact that what you are reading is all just a bunch of fiction. Fantasyland! There is no Hollywood here, no truth, no artistic integrity. I make no claim to be writing, or even attempting to write, pulp fiction (a fanciful little misnomer that conceals the fact that really it is the purest of truth, Hollywood made flesh—or at least, logos); neither its cultured cousin modern literature (haute pulp, as for the most part I see and venerate it). No, this is just dross and, although there is always that risk that it could fall into the wrong hands and be used for the base entertainment of society's more questionable elements, I offer it up to you, dear Reader, as an example of vice to be used as such in the furtherance of virtue. Not once—to my shame here, and I freely confess it—will you get from me the pirouette crash, that Old Faithful of vehicular action; never a phonecall-incognito-limited-to-thirty-seconds-so-as-to-evade-location-identification (whatever urge led you to suspect that this particular manifestation of truth is merely a device of the lazy, by the lazy and for the lazy needs to be suppressed this very minute, Reader); nor any other of the million little viewing details that make the most licentious among us scream out in our—I mean, their—licentious exasperation. And I am not even touching on the more fundamental and all-encompassing truths that can be gleaned from an awareness, understanding and acceptance (or, conversely and more typically, through unthinking subliminal ingestion) of the great themes consistently underlying the standard fare with which Hollywood blesses us.

Let this, then, be a warning to the wise, Reader—and a disclaimer to the litigious.

Chapter 5

Discretion, the existential responsibility of genuine discretion. This is the foundation of any island, lacking which you will slide into the sea and drown. It is such a huge subject that I hardly know where to begin. In tackling it I might as well be tackling the whole ten months just past, both large aspects and small. I suspect, therefore, that this is going to be a very long chapter, Reader. But it won't be tedious—that's for sure! Anything but tedious. So maybe you want to go get yourself some popcorn or otherwise prepare yourself for the long haul. I'm really not kidding. This could be a hundred pages or more—and I expect you to read this chapter, like any other, all in one sitting. You and your television-fed attention span. (I didn't hear any whining about the length of Chapter One, now did I?)

Let me begin by telling you how I saw one of my brothers there in Mazatlán—and not just once, but three times. This experience was an exercise in discretion, and I mean that it really exercised me and mine. Knowledge and awareness are important elements of discretion, but more important yet is simple willpower. The first time I saw Sep he was getting on the bus. "Aaaaah, Ai'm prud o' ye, laddy," was my instant thought—the guy lives on a

50-foot yacht and there he was pinching his centavos taking the public transit. (We MacOlsons are a frugal tribe, one and all.) With all the racket and commotion he was making just getting on the bus, it was obvious that discretion was a non-issue for Sep (short for Septimus). Even had he not had to brutalize the bus-driver for information in what some guidebook had led him to believe was Spanish, he would still have stuck out like a sore thumb. Mexicans are not blond, for one thing, nor do they have blue eyes, for another—at least, not the ones who take the bus; but most importantly, being in their own element they simply do not draw attention. That is a macro-aspect of discretion, Reader: making whatever element you are in your own element—enough, at least, so that you do not draw attention.

I saw Sep, but he didn't see me. Why? First of all, my hair is currently black, Mexican black. Although this is only a couple shades darker than my natural brown, it makes all the difference as to blending in. To a Mexican, and rightly so in this context, a rubio is a rubio whether he is flaxen blond or chestnut brown. When black is the standard, everything else is unique, whether less so or more so. Then, to go with my black hair I have a deep tan, deep enough for me to pass here as a guero, a fair-skinned Latino. And as far as my dress is concerned, you know already that it is not a flower-print shirt and Bermuda shorts. (I should note that I was relieved to see what Sep was wearing—not, rather—and neither was he sunburnt!) I always dress unostentatiously, jeans and some bland shirt, usually long-sleeved. This means that there are only two elements of my apparel that are genuine disguise devices, and these are my baseball cap and my sunglasses. There is no simpler yet more effective disguise than a baseball cap and shades—social levelers that turn every one of us into just another goober.

When Sep saw me—I'm saying, when his eyes took in his surroundings on that bus—I was wearing my shades and baseball cap and I would have been facing out the window like any other bus-rider. (Face someone squarely and you will attract their attention almost as certainly as if you had glanced directly at them because our brains are wired so that we are incredibly sensitive to eyes monitoring our own or faces positioned such that the eyes they contain are likely to be monitoring us). So Sep did not see me, even though he was within two feet of me as he passed down the aisle and found an empty seat on the other side three rows back. We then rode like that till he got off. I faced away from him the whole time and monitored him entirely by ear (which was not difficult in the least). Anyone other than a family member or close friend and I would have been comfortable with a couple brief, indirect glances to the side in addition.

If my primary purpose in coming to Mazatlán was to see Sep (I didn't tell you that yet, Reader? Well, I'm telling you now!), why did I not take this opportunity to make contact with him? What better place, if one is concerned about surveillance or apprehension, would there be to meet with somebody than on a bus in México, or at the bus-stop immediately afterwards? I mean, there could hardly be a better place, especially for someone on the budget I'm on. The problem, though, was that Sep wasn't alone. He had his best friend in tow. This really threw me off balance. What was Todd doing here? He had his drafting firm and eighteen children (and counting) back in Calgary to be taking care of. He didn't need to be running around Mazatlán, my Mazatlán, ogling all these hot Mexican chicas, my hot Mexican chicas with their micro-minis and stilettos, with their glossy black hair, their warm brown eyes and their seventeen inch waists, and with their perfect-physiques-resulting-from-an-active-walking-lifestyle-absent-car-transportation. (Man, oh man! What am I thinking, leaving this place? Is it too late to turn this ferry around? Am I a strong enough swimmer to reach that rapidly receding shoreline?!?)

I didn't actually care about not being able to initiate contact with Sep there on the bus. I came to Mazatlán to see him, but I had not gotten on that bus with any plans or expectations to see him there. Something as momentous as a meeting like this—

momentous to a discreet traveler like myself—really needs proper preparation, both mental and circumstantial. Had Todd not been accompanying Sep, I would have approached him (upon disembarking), but I would nevertheless have felt a little uneasy about doing so in a setting and according to timing not entirely of my own design.

I was actually a little surprised to see that Sep was in town. I had been in Mazatlán for two or three weeks at that point and I had scouted around the three marinas regularly but had found no sign of him. My information before traveling to this place was that he was expected to reach here around the end of January. Bad information, obviously. That's par for the course when discretion is your polestar. It was this consideration for discretion that necessitated my reliance—I guess "reliance" isn't exactly the best term when you are doing anything but relying—for information on my lawyer, Lucifer Lewretch.

Let me tell you, Reader, just a little about Lewretch. (In case you are wondering, I think his name is French, or at least Anglo-Norman from the pronunciation). Lewretch is everything a lawyer could ever hope to be. When you think the word "lawyer" and imagine all the connotations, positive and negative (that is, the positive one—whatever it may be—and all the others, the entire unnumbered host), you are thinking of, you are picturing in your mind, Lewretch, bless his soul. The first time I spoke to Lewretch I had yet to set eyes on him. I was calling him from a pay booth in Victoria. Just moments before that, as I had been trudging along the road toward the old-fashioned little corner store where the pay booth was, an oncoming cop car had slowed down in passing and I could feel the cop's eyes on me. Fortunately I had had my baseball cap and shades on, and the entirety of my possessions (excluding my kayak and camping supplies down on the shore at the bottom of a nearby cliff)—which I was carrying in my hand—consisted of merely one scholarly-looking, full knapsack. So I passed that little test. The cop's inquisitiveness may have been mostly my imagination, but I was very concerned at the time because some days earlier I had made an indiscreet phone call from that general area. Anyway, let me tell you, that brief encounter with a police car was nothing compared to the chill that went down my spine moments later just hearing the sound of Lewretch's voice. Every lawyer has that lawyerly hiss; they study and learn it in first year law, along with bombast, sophistry and dissemblance. Unless you are unfamiliar with lawyers at first hand, Reader, you know exactly what I'm talking about. But you've never heard a hiss like Lewretch's hiss. It was as if a forty foot long boa constrictor had slithered out of the phone and wrapped itself around me, head to toe. That was the first time I called Lewretch; but it's been no different any other time—I've just learned since how to control the knocking of my knees and keep from allowing his glittering eyes to mesmerize me into a state of total helplessness.

So Lewretch had told me at the beginning of January that Sep was sailing to Mazatlán and that he was keeping an eye out for me on his travels hoping to run into me. I had heard earlier from Lewretch, back in August before I had had to cut him off for awhile, about Sep wanting to meet with me, but back then I had been too preoccupied with keeping body and soul together to consider taking any little detour to the south that was sure to end in a lecture and a sermon if nothing else. This time I had a little cash in my pocket, besides which I figured that I had been out traveling long enough to demonstrate that I was perfectly capable of managing to survive and thrive under the strained circumstances I was in—meaning that when I turn myself in it will be by choice and not in desperation, something I consider important for my future jury to understand. And by all that I mean that I know that Sep, although I'm sure he tells himself he wants to help me and will not try to force my decision in any way, will have a one-track mind when I see him about getting me to turning myself in. I would not be here on this ferry leaving Mazatlán to find him in La Paz if I were not already prepared to do that very thing.

All of life is a negotiation, Reader. Negotiation, incessant negotiation. It's unavoidable. The refusal to negotiate is nothing but a form or tactic of negotiation, whether the refusenik knows it or not, or accepts it or not. Discretion, especially in circumstances like these that I'm in, frequently necessitates reliance on questionable or incomplete information. In this it is very similar to negotiation. It is the ideal of every negotiator to be in complete possession of all the information pertinent to the negotiation, including such things as the parameters of his opponent's bargaining position; but the reality is that such is virtually never the case.

In the interests of discretion, I had come to México relying on information from Lewretch that I would find Sep there in Mazatlán in late January. I knew that this information was not necessarily the best. My family will talk to Lewretch now and then, but it isn't regular contact. When I talk to him myself it is always just out of the blue (from his perspective), and it is out of the question for me to give him any opportunity to check or update information. As for me making direct contact with anyone in possession of better information, that is even more out of the question. Not knowing what level of interest the authorities have in me, subsequently what degree of surveillance aimed at my apprehension that my family and friends might be under, I have to assume the worst reasonable. Although it is obvious that the resources of the authorities are finite, my lack of sophistication in this sphere necessitates the assumption of super-competence on their part. They can fail a hundred times and succeed once, and they win. I have to succeed all one hundred and one times, like the Dalmatians, just to keep from losing. Regarding communication, all of this means that I absolutely cannot make any phone calls to the home phones (or cell phones) of my family or friends. I must assume that these are highly monitored. Nor can I make long distance calls to their workplaces; local calls may be okay to unassigned phones at a large employer (although then the risk arises as to the person who answers the phone initially and must be trusted to locate whoever I would be looking for), but long distance calls, particularly ones made from pay phones or other unusual locations, certainly are at risk of raising a red flag placed with the phone company. Maybe you think I am being paranoid here, Reader. You may be right, but some level of paranoia is essential in these circumstances. I have been told that last summer one of my sisters, who is a sales rep for a cosmetics company, was tailed all day one day as she traveled from client to client, and that a few days after that a couple of my little nieces had to go out to their front sidewalk with their water-pistols and gun down some guy who had been loitering at the edge of my brother's property for over an hour clearly surveilling the premises. I can also, and will later, tell you about a close scrape I myself had in the fall, a scrape possibly engendered by the letting down of my guard for only a moment, a seemingly harmless instant of time.

Let's get back now to Sep in Mazatlán. As I said, I am now on the ferry to go see him in La Paz. Why, you are wondering, Reader, must I go see him in La Paz when I could just as easily—I mean, way more easily—have seen him in Mazatlán? Well, the first time I saw him, there on the bus with his buddy Todd, contact was out of the question. Todd is a good guy, mind you, and I would not distrust him in the least, fear betrayal at his hands, that is, but I'm not going to put some bystander, some civilian, out there like that. Mere contact with myself—not aiding me or hiding me or encouraging me in any way, but merely coming into contact with me—in the situation I'm in and the poor guy would be left conflicted. I am as much of a pariah in our society as a leper would have been in ancient Palestine or an excommunicant in medieval Europe.

The second time I saw Sep was at a bullfight. Have you ever seen a bullfight, Reader? The bullring in Mazatlán looks like a coliseum, round, steep and full of dust and heat. (Maybe not dust, but it felt like it with dirt being the only alternative inside there from concrete). The cheap seats are on the side where the sun beats down fiercest, but it's fierce everywhere in there. I'm not Hemingway, so I couldn't give a care about the bullfight itself. Really just a bunch of BF, if you ask me. (Ha, ha, ha! Laugh, Reader, laugh! At least smile!) Anyway, first a guy on a horse wears the poor beast down for a while and then, and only then, does the matador come out to show off his prowess. There is probably a lot more skill involved than what it appears, but I was unimpressed. It looked like a one-sided affair to me. I really did find myself cheering for the bull, hopeless as his struggle inevitably must be. There was an amusing part where a bunch of guys (bricklayers, I suppose) line up and the bull charges them. The first guy takes the bull head on and clings to him as he plows on to the rest. This continues so that eventually half a dozen guys have grappled on and the bull stops and falls down with their combined weight. I would describe it all to you a little better if I could, Reader, but none of it compared to the chica I had there with me, Yesenia, and so all that bullfighting is nothing more to me than a dusty haze in my memory.

Yesenia! ... Ahuy! (As they say in México—or is it "Ajai"?) That girl is fine. Like so many Mazatlecas, she is just a perfect specimen of femininity. (I'm telling you, the place is a New Jerusalem). I met her at Olas Altas, a small beach by the coolest part of Old Mazatlán. Not that she is the type of girl to hang out around the tourist bars and all that. Yesenia is a good girl from a proper family. She was sitting on the seawall just above the beach waiting the few minutes until it would be time for her to go to class, her English class. Although she was not inviting conversation, the chance to practice her English with a real Anglophone, especially just before class, was ideal.

This isn't a romance I'm writing here, Reader, so forget about Yesenia. She came and went. The same is true for every other girl I have gotten to know this past year, and there have been a lot of them. Traveling like this seems to be a good context for putting yourself into circulation. On the other hand, traveling like this necessitates an overwhelming superficiality in relationships. If you are someone who values momentary gratification—and I am not, besides which, I do take seriously the risk of nasty diseases—then this might just be the life for you, really. I make no claim to studliness. I am just an average guy. Yet, as often as not this past year the women I have come into contact with have been all but falling over themselves trying to get with me. I, for my part, in many cases have reciprocated just as enthusiastically, but where the women have been able to engage freely, I am inevitably brought up short by discretion and its dictates. I am like the dog in Sylvester and Tweety who is always chasing Sylvester and then, coming to the end of his leash, gets yanked up short for, like, the ninetieth time. Even at this very moment, as I am sitting here on this ferry, there is another pretty girl—not as pretty as Yesenia—with beautiful green eyes back there in Mazatlán wondering what she could have done in another way to make me stay, and hoping beyond hope for a call, or even just a postcard, from Montana, my home state, you know, to which I am now returning.

So I saw Sep a second time at the bullfight and you know, Reader, that even apart from the fact that he was there with a bunch of friends, I was not going to be initiating contact between us, not with a distraction like Yesenia on my arm, not with Yesenia's hesitant English caressing my ears and her languid brown eyes monopolizing my mind.

By that time Sep must have been in Mazatlán a couple weeks. (I assume that he had been there only a couple days when I had first seen him on the bus because I had been keeping fairly good track of the marinas). The bullfight had been on a Sunday afternoon. Toward the end of that week I moseyed on out to the marina he was at in hopes of finally establishing contact with him there. By then I had figured out that it was actually possible to telephone the marinas and get information, to some extent, and unreliably so, that way.

This third close encounter with Sep is a good demonstration of the function of willpower in discretion. I am still debating within myself whether or not I made the right decision that day. (If I don't catch up to him in La Paz, then I guess I'll know). The marina he was at was located at basically the north end of Mazatlán. The whole northern section of Mazatlán is all touristy. It's called the Golden Triangle. That marina is quite large and it has a nice cobblestone walk following the water's edge and giving access to the docks. As I wandered down this walkway toward the docks I wondered how I would be able to figure out which boat was Sep's. I knew the boat's name, so I figured I would just ask someone if I had to, but I really didn't want to become committed like that. It would have looked odd, I'm sure, to make such an inquiry and then not necessarily follow up on it by hailing the owners themselves. As it turned out, my concern there was groundless. Sep's boat was the first in line. He had his flag—the only Canadian flag I could see—fluttering proudly and I confirmed the identification with a peek at the boat's name.

Listen, Reader, I trust Sep. I know him well enough to know that he will readily stoop to emotional blackmail, but beyond that he will not try to compel my decision as to turning myself in. So my hesitation there at the marina was not on that score. (Oh—I forgot to say: instead of stepping out on the dock and approaching Sep's boat, I sat down on a bench close by looking out across the water.) Nobody was astir in his boat—that was one thing. Another was simply that I had come to see Sep, and only Sep. His wife is a sweet girl and I would have no trepidation about trusting her, but doing so would necessarily be a violation of discretion. Along with that consideration was the fact that, for all I knew, Todd was still there or some other guest may have appeared. So, in sitting down on that bench, I was basically just trying to get the lie of the land.

It was late morning when I arrived at Sep's marina and had a seat by the water's edge. The sun, as always on this coast, was warm but not fierce. This was a couple months ago. (Did I mention that?) The marina is distant from the bulk of Mazatlán and so it is quiet enough there for the loudest sound to be the steady under-rhythm of the breakers on the beaches nearby. It wasn't long before I heard some noises from Sep's boat and he and his wife appeared on deck. They got off the boat onto the dock and then from there they stepped ashore. They walked right past me. My bench was between the walk and the water, so I wasn't actually facing them, but I was very, very available for viewing. Why didn't they recognize me? That was partly chance, to be sure; however, discretion was a factor, too. I was sitting there calmly, fitting into the scenery, not drawing attention in any way. I had a prop, a book that I was apparently reading, but otherwise—apart from my ever present baseball cap and shades—I was completely on display. It was probably a good thing that I had that book, because marinas are very chummy places and their etiquette may very well demand polite exchanges in such situations absent obvious preoccupation on the part of one or the other party.

Discretion was a factor in this non-exchange not only tactically, but strategically as well. Being very conscious of the possibility of Sep's not being alone, I was fully prepared to return another day (another and another) and try my luck again (again and again). Contacting him was my primary reason for coming to Mazatlán; hence doing so, and doing so in the manner of my choosing, was my priority. I was not fretting about getting away from there in a rush. (As a matter of fact, I had a secondary reason for being in Mazatlán, and that was that it seemed a good place to cool my heels while waiting for Lewretch to try one last time to arrange for the charge against me to be dropped and the arrest warrant withdrawn. However, it appears now that he has been unable to do so.) The long and short is that, although it was a real temptation, sister-in-law or no, just to walk up to my brother, say hello and give him a hug—discretion dictated otherwise. So you can see, Reader, that, although knowledge and awareness are necessary elements in discretion, simple willpower is the keystone when it comes to the crunch.

Chapter 6

Tired of discretion yet, Reader? Me too. Let's let our hair down a little. (Or not).

This epistle is about being an island. You figured that out, right? No man is an island, and all that. I was going to title it 'On Being an Island', but that sounded a little long-winded. I'll have to check and see if Huxley beat me to it, but I kind of recall a "the" in his.

I am an island. Well, I am as much of an island as anyone ever gets, any normal person. I would describe my attainment of this status as a three-part process. The first step came with my leaving Calgary abruptly last June. I had just barely arrived and then I suddenly left. Reaching island status was not my intent then in any way. In my perspective I was merely sequestering myself temporarily while the matter leading to such sequestration sorted itself out. Well, obviously, it didn't—and it still hasn't, more's the pity.

Camping. I wasn't traveling then. I was camping. Before leaving Calgary I called my best friend and asked him to lend me some money. When he asked me how much, I told him that just whatever was convenient would be fine, having in mind that he would stop at a bank machine after work to pick up some cash. I figured three or four hundred bucks—that's about the maximum withdrawal from a machine, isn't it?—would suffice for a few weeks out in the bush. I may be a city boy, but I've spent a fair bit of time in the great outdoors and I'm comfortable out there with the bare essentials, relatively speaking. Anyway, what my friend went and did shows you what a good guy he is: without having any insight as to my situation apart from the facts that I had just arrived unexpectedly in Calgary and this was the only time I had ever asked him for a loan, he leaves work early so as to get to his bank during business hours and clean out his savings account. When I saw him—this was late in the afternoon that day—and he handed me more than two thousand dollars, hard earned dollars, I was really floored, and filled with gratitude. As if that wasn't more than enough, he then offered to go after his term deposits saying that it would take a few days on that because of the bank's restrictions. I'm glad that that was out of the question for me. Really, I felt bad accepting even the whole wad of cash he had brought for me. That there, Reader, is a true friend—and a real man: ready to help when the chips are down, yet demanding no word of explanation.

Camping was an interesting experience. Of course, camping always is interesting for the urbanite—that's why the government makes sure there are a lot of long weekends through the summer months. But this little camping trip of mine was particularly interesting on account of the mindset I had. I felt tentatively cut off from society. It was my hope that the immediate course of events would result in a reconciliation between society and me, but as things stood the relationship was in a state of limbo, limbo at best. Besides feeling cut off from society, I felt pursued. Looking back now, I'm sure that I was getting a little carried away there. The issuing of an arrest warrant, momentous as it is to the typical bourgeois, really is a far cry from the mounting of a full-blown manhunt. But it was a sense of the latter that dogged my thoughts throughout my entire camping phase. I suppose a big part of that is the innate egocentrism that any of us has and that causes a person to divide reality, at some primal level, between self and everything else—or, in a social context, between self and everyone else. Most of us likely never confront this within ourselves because modern life insulates us so very well from the more primal levels of being, but the closer to an island one becomes, the more one's insulation is torn away.

What do you know about bears, Reader? They're cuddly and cute, right? And so roly-poly and friendly. You've seen koalas on TV sedately chewing away on eucalyptus leaves, or pandas eating bamboo shoots, or maybe polar bears sliding along on the ice having a grand old time. They really are nothing other than overgrown stuffed toys. They even dance, for heaven's sake.

Well, I hate to have to be the one to break it to you, Reader, but bears are monsters. I'd take Freddie Krueger any day over a bear. Modern technology shields us from this truth about bears, but take it away—the modern technology—and if you find yourself in close confrontation with a bear you will very quickly realize that the only thing that had put and kept you higher on the food chain than him was that technology. The bear is a monster. Even his name, bear, bears witness to his monstrosity. Our ancestors had a different word for bear, but they were so afraid of bears that they refused even to say this word and it became taboo. You know, don't even mention the unmentionable terror and maybe it will go away for good—or at least you will keep the fear from being debilitating. But they had to refer to bears somehow—the subject was not entirely avoidable—so, instead of discussing them by name, they just obliquely referred to "the brown ones". "Brown", therefore, is the source of our word "bear", similarly "bruin".

So, are we clear on bears, Reader? They are not cuddly and cute, except on TV. And they are not roly-poly and friendly. They are monsters and, given the right circumstances, they will readily eat your friendly carcass. You think I'm kidding? A friend of mine has been a volunteer with search-and-rescue in BC for a couple years or so now. There was a call recently from the family of some hunters who were late by a day or two in returning from their hunt. This is wild country we're talking about, rugged wilderness high in the mountains, just the other side of the continental divide from Banff. So my friend joins the search team and they set out. One group goes up the trail the hunters took while a second group, including my friend, is taken up by chopper to a point high on the mountain to follow the trail down. Fortunately for my friend and his companions, snow flurries caused poor visibility and nixed any landing at the higher elevation up there. Why do I say "fortunately"? Because bears are monsters. Listen to me, Reader. Reality still exists outside of our little cocoons, our globalized little übercocoon, and one aspect of it that you will almost certainly never have to confront is that bears genuinely are monsters. The chopper then followed the trail down and the group inside spotted the best they could from in there for the hunters or any sight of them. About halfway down they came upon them, their remains. A mother silver-tip grizzly and her two full-grown cubs had killed the men. The bears were still there feeding on the hunters' remains.

If a bear is a monster—and it is!—then the grizzly bear is the monster of all monsters. I won't pretend like I'm any kind of an expert on grizzlies, Reader, but you have to understand that a Calgary native like myself can't help but have considerably more exposure to the subject than your average person. The grizzly's habitat has been so reduced that Calgary is the only major city still within close proximity to a sizable and viable grizzly habitat. This makes Calgary the center of grizzly studies, and it means that the region's hikers and outdoorsmen have considerable knowledge of the animals.

I have never seen a grizzly in the wild. Few people have. But I have seen and heard about what they can do. When I was a kid I saw a picture in the Calgary Herald of a truck that had been parked on the side of a highway when a grizzly found it and smelled food inside. Bears are so clever that the national parks service has had to devise special garbage dumpsters with latching lids so as to keep them from getting in—and even then they still sometimes manage to break in. This bear with the truck though, being a grizzly, wasn't wasting his time with all that Harry Houdini cleverness. He got his claws into an edge of the door frame and he just pulled and bent until he'd opened up the truck can-opener style. The thing looked like it had been in an accident, and all it was was a hungry grizzly.

I'm telling you all this about bears, Reader, because when I left Calgary I hitchhiked out to Banff and started my camping expedition from there. And there had apparently been a number of bad maulings last spring because there were special bear warning signs posted everywhere. The campground that I got the hippie and his girlfriend in a Volkswagen Westphalia—yes, really, a Volkswagen Westphalia, and with a resident canine that seemed to feed mainly on vehicle upholstery—to drop me at was so deserted (this is highly unusual for late June) that they thought I was nuts to ignore all these signs.

What was I thinking to head into a bear zone like that. Was it because I am brave? That is, does this mean that I'm brave? Not necessarily, Reader. I have often wondered what bravery is, even when on one of those rare occasions that I am actually doing something nominally brave. According to the Arthurian ideal, which has been wholeheartedly adopted and expounded by Hollywood, a courageous man acting courageously is temporarily blinded to danger. He laughs at danger. That arrow sticking out of his posterior? A mere pinprick. Remind him to pluck it out when the battle is over. Alone and surrounded by a hundred Apaches? What—only a hundred? Bring 'em on! And make it quick because he's got a poker game and a girl waiting on him at the saloon in town.

It seems to me that there are two—at least two—kinds of bravery. (I am thinking out loud here, so feel free, Reader, to mentally interject your own thoughts at any time and refine or correct what I am expressing). The one is essentially hormonal. You just get carried away and do something entirely heedlessly. And almost inevitably you look back on your actions after and you think to yourself that whatever you just did was really stupid, that you took unreasonable—and, often as not, entirely unnecessary—risks. Bravery of this nature is little if nothing more than fearlessness, the absence of fear. Yet, if fear is a natural thing (and when I say natural, I imply good), if our various fear mechanisms are long-ingrained and highly developed response protocols to a host of dangers, known and unknown, then for us to shut them down or indiscriminately override them involves a diminution of our mental capacity, a diminution of self. This leads me to conclude that such hormonal bravery is essentially animalistic. Therefore, outwardly milk my own such exploits for all they are worth (and for so much more actually) though I might, do and will, inwardly all I can sincerely do in response to such actions of mine is raise my eyebrows and slowly shake my head.

The other kind of bravery is far more interesting. However, it has the drawback of not fitting the Hollywood stereotype in the least (which, granted, relegates it in our black-and-white society to non-bravery, also known as cowardice). This form of bravery acknowledges fear, fears, at all times; and, instead of ignoring them, it heeds them. However, in heeding fears it does not necessarily act in accordance with their proddings. Sometimes it does, but sometimes it doesn't. Basically it treats fears as factors to be considered along with facts and objectives and everything else in the decision process. In dangerous situations with perils at every turn, that process is reduced pretty much to the juggling of fears, their constant prioritization and re-prioritization all within a matter of minutes, sometimes even seconds. So, at times, this second kind of bravery could be best described as calculated cowardice. And that is how I perceive my solitary wanderings in bear country: as calculated cowardice, a juggling of fears. (Bear in mind, of course, that only a heretic, an anti-Hollywood like myself, could countenance and nurture such shamelessness within himself).

When I got out of that hippie wagon and bid farewell to the hippies, all three of them, at a campground in the lee of Castle Mountain, I was glad to be on my own. I felt like Bilbo Baggins in the Hobbit as he set out from Hobbiton. It was great to be out in the mountains with the rich, clean air filling my lungs. Best of all, I had the whole place all to myself.

As the sound of the departing vehicle faded into the distance and silence descended I took my bearings. It must have been the longest day of the year because it was still light out, but soon now the sun would be setting and the darkness would fall like a heavy curtain. Nighttime in the forest is a hundred times darker than on the prairie. Unless there is a moon or you've got a flashlight, you're not going anywhere. Another bear warning sign caught my eye. Bilbo gave a little shiver. It's always cool in the mountains. He—I mean, I—suddenly noticed how deathly quiet it was there in that big, empty parking lot surrounded by tall, dark evergreens. We had the whole place entirely to ourself. Yikes!

Giving himself a little shake and chuckling at himself, Braveheart quickly set out on a trail leading up the mountain. It wasn't even a proper trail, in fact, because I didn't want to run into any other hikers. It was a strange time of day to be heading upstream and so this would have caused real curiosity. Knowing that bears generally prefer to avoid people and that most encounters with them result from surprising them, I sang as I hiked. My initial selections were routine camping fare like Bingo and Old MacDonald. After a while, though, as the twilight really began to set in, I plucked a hymnal out of thin air and commenced with the sacred. Not only was I going to alert the bears to my presence, but I was also going to shame them for plotting to eat an innocent wayfarer like myself. The sinners!

Castle Mountain is north of the TransCanada near the Radium turn-off. The old highway, the 1A, skirts it. I'm actually a little hazy on its name. I think the original name was Castle Mountain, and that probably because it looks like one; and I think it has reverted back to that name. However, when I was in Grade Six and my class camped in the near vicinity and went for a day hike up it, I know that it was called Mt. Eisenhower. I figure it was renamed after World War Two in honor of the American general who played such an important role in our eventual victory, and I'm all for honoring those whose prowess or sacrifices have safeguarded our homeland, be they Western Canadian or not. At the same time I respect those more localized traditionalists who wish to maintain things as they are, the name of this mountain in this instance. (Of course, I am making a couple assumptions here that may be completely wrong. Oh well!) Anyway, the mountain kind of runs northwest to southeast, and it is gargantuan. It has wooded slopes that rise to a steep wall. Nearing this wall the slopes turn into scree and the trees thin out considerably. Above the wall, which is a thousand feet or so high, it is quite steep terrain and from a distance it looks mostly like scree slope made of debris crumbled off the central massif rising high into the sky. It really amazes me when I stop to think about it like this what breathtakingly wondrous beauty I grew up around and how I have always taken such beauty for granted as if everyone everywhere were so blest. The more I have traveled and become acquainted with different peoples and places, the more I have come to recognize how precious a treasure Calgary is, Calgary and environs: the people and the place.

I got maybe halfway to the wall when the twilight deepened too much for further travel that night. It was still heavily wooded where I was, but the slope was already getting steep enough that I had to scout around to find somewhere suitable to stretch out my sleeping bag. The best I could do was to jam myself against a fallen tree trunk that was held firmly in place by the healthy trees it was wedged against. If you think that sounds uncomfortable, Reader, you are absolutely right. Dog-tired though I was, I hardly slept through the night.

So, what was I doing on the top of Castle Mountain anyway (okay, maybe a quarter of the way up, but as toppish as I was going to get with that thousand foot wall blocking any further ascent)? That is a good question. And I mean, once I did get up there the following morning I paused for a while to collect my wits. My primary objective was to make myself entirely unavailable for a couple weeks or so. Remember, Reader, I was camping at this point, not traveling. This allowed me to pursue even more complete isolation—temporarily—than is necessary or desirable for a permanent island. Looking down over the Bow Valley and across to the mountains rising on the other side of it, I could hear the eighteen-wheelers on the TransCanada four or five miles distant from my perch. Each truck had a distinctive shhhh and roar as it wended along, mostly or entirely hidden from me by the tall lodgepole pines skirting the highway. I was glad to have put such separation between me and civilization. This was about the right amount; any more was entirely unnecessary and would require considerably more preparation or commitment. Yet, my present location was problematic. I was indeed nervous about the bears. A day or two of risk (apparent risk, at least) is a rush; but did I really want to have to stay on edge like this for the next two or three weeks? And, although I had put some distance between Calgary and myself, I was still definitely in the vicinity. If any widespread effort were to be taken to apprehend me then I was no less vulnerable here from chance encounters with observant people than if I had remained in the city itself. Even the bear situation was a two-edged sword: while it served to keep people out of the forest and off the hiking trails, thus providing me with some readymade and welcome privacy, it naturally left any remaining hikers like myself exposed and brought us into sharp distinction. As a matter of fact, I never saw a single other hiker in the few days I spent around there, but if I had run into anyone else out there, do you think that I could have just silently walked past them or gotten away with a brief greeting? Of course not! I would have had to stop and chat and listen to warnings about the bears, if nothing else. And then, when this person got back to the city and saw or read the news, my whereabouts would have been immediately narrowed down to the spot where we had met, plus maybe a ten or twenty mile radius.

I didn't come to any conclusion that day as to my next move. I did follow the base of the mountain's wall to the northwest with the vague intention of circling to the backside and deeper bush there, but it was really slow going on that terrain and I didn't get far by the time the day was over. I made myself a better nest that night than the previous one. I didn't get much sleep, however, because sometime in the middle of the night I was disturbed—frightened—by the sound of a large, dry branch breaking somewhere within a hundred yards or so of where I lay, a branch at least two inches in diameter. I never heard any accompanying sounds—you can bet, Reader, that I was listening then—and so for a little while I tried to explain it away, but I couldn't come up with anything too convincing, so I just got scared and ended up crawling into a tree with my sleeping bag and trying to get a little peace of mind (and rest) there. What I got instead—fool I was for thinking I could sleep in an 8,000-year-old pricklecone pine—was a lovely and memorable view of a midsummer's dawn from the top of the Canadian Rockies, not a bad exchange at all for a bit of sleep. Even an island can appreciate the beauty of a sunrise.

Chapter 7

I think I'll leave you stranded on Castle Mountain surrounded by ravenous grizzlies for a while, Reader. It'll be a good experience for you. More to the point, I caught myself slipping into a chronological narrative. That is so Hollywood. Reduce everything to the simplest terms possible and present it all in some nice, straightforward configuration. That won't confuse all those highly discriminating lowest-common-denominators out there who have been so kind as to pay their admission and be sucked into shelling out a 2000% mark-up for popcorn and carbonated corn syrup. Well, I've got news for you, Cecil B. DeVille: existence may be inarguably monochronic, but our perception of it is anything but. So if you want authenticity in your narrative—and that is a really good thing from many points of view, particularly the propagandistic—then you need to drop the monolithicity from your drama and be like Bose speakers with their sound layering. Our perception—and effective communication is all about transmitting the perception-set contained within one mind to another mind—is like that sound layering in reverse: an event occurs and we perceive it; then we perceive it again, whether in some other way or in light of different aspects than those which guided us in our initial perception; and we accordingly perceive it again and again with mostly diminishing such reverberations. Yet, unlike the reverberations in Bose's sound layering, those of perception are entirely polychronic, skipping from her voice to her eyes and to the clear blue sky all in an instant even though, chronologically, the sky was there and steady throughout and you had looked into her eyes and held her gaze prior to her uttering a single word (that as an example).

This topic of perception reminds me of the concept for a sitcom that came to me when I was living in LA. (Living on the streets of Hollywood, to be precise—I must have been inspired by my surroundings). I have been playing with this stupid thing on and off ever since and I'm still not sure if its fundamental logic is possible. I'll think I've got a workable configuration going, but then some fissure appears and all but instantaneously causes a blowout of such massive proportions that my poor little three pounds of gray matter is left quivering and twitching for a week and skittish as a schoolgirl about taking up the cursed thing again. Really, I should just abandon the concept and cut my losses on it—but I can't seem to, my precious doesn't seem to want me to let it go.

'TVeality'. That's what I have named it. It's whacked. I'm warning you, Reader. The logic is not entirely there, and may ultimately be impossible. I hope for your sake that you can just skim over this in a noncommittal way and keep from the insidious and relentless mental entanglement I find myself in here. It's torture. (And you'd better not solve this Gordian quagmire on me! It's my mess, I tell you! Keep your non-Euclidean grubs to yourself! My precious has eyes only for me!)

Okay, so this guy, Ted, appears in the pilot show of a new sitcom. The show is set in a television studio. It's about the internal workings of the studio. Ted has just been hired as a director's assistant, and the only reason he was hired is that his uncle is one of the main shareholders in the company that owns the studio. Well, here's my logic problem, and problematic as it is, it's also exquisitely delicious: the show that Ted's new boss is directing is the same that we are in fact watching. 'TVeality'. Isn't that delectable, Reader? (Run! Fly! Get away while you are yet able!) And, as the icing on the cake, Ted is with us; he's on our side; he's the only person on the show who knows it's a show. Or more accurately, he's the only person on the show who knows and admits that it's a show. The others play it entirely straight the whole time, and worse yet, they seem to constantly whisper behind Ted's—and, by extension, our—back about how crazy and paranoid and delusional he is, and they are constantly—or, at least, appear to be constantly—scheming about how to get rid of him.

(I warned you, Reader. Don't say I never did. I did. Maybe if you're fortunate you are dense enough that this hasn't clicked with you. In which case you can just thank your lucky stars and scurry onward, leaving the metaphysics to nuts like Ted and me.)

Like any other sitcom, 'TVeality' is episodic. I've sketched out a fair number of episodes. In the pilot everything starts out perfectly normal and perfectly Hollywood, every single imaginable cliché thrown in—yes, the PC in particular—but not done too gratuitously or self-consciously. It's just another sitcom and the ostensible subject matter is the workings in general of a television studio. Ted is playing his role like everyone else, until about two thirds of the way through. The one normalism that is overdone a little is the laughter of the studio audience, and this occurs start to finish—but it is overdone only a little, not enough that it is definitely notable to us viewers without the confirmation Ted will give it. However, there is one laugher in this audience who has a distinctive, goofy laugh and who gets progressively louder as the show goes on. Finally, at about two thirds of the way through, some poorly scripted joke is made—something that deserves as little laughter as 80% of the jokes in your average sitcom deserve—and the audience laughs as usual with the goofy-laugher really going off, loud and long. Ted, who had been starting to seem a little off for the previous few minutes, a little exasperated and increasingly so, loses it. He yells at the guy to shut up and the whole studio audience goes silent. Then he starts ranting and raving about the mediocrities of the show, starting with studio audience handling and then moving on to all the clichés we've been watching. As his fellow actors watch and listen to him, he turns on them, criticizing them fiercely for being such sheep. However, they remain noncommittal and refuse to interact with him on this level. Their ambiguity is key to the show's success. We, the viewers, must be able to interpret their actions in either of two ways: that they are actors sticking to their roles in spite of Ted's tantrum; or that they are studio staff looking on a crazy man and not wanting to stimulate any heightened aggression in him. This fundamental ambiguity must be maintained for the entire life of the show because it is what makes the show (yet its logic is what is driving me up the wall here). Anyway, after ranting for a while and continuing to get such indulgent ambiguity from his fellow actors, Ted gets even more frustrated and argumentative in a let's-cut-the-crap-here-for-a-minute kind of way. He starts pointing out the cameras and the studio audience, but when one of the cameras pans around to follow his gestures there are no other cameras there and no studio audience, just the other end of the office or whatever room that scene is in. The camera action here is crucial, and again the logic involved is problematic at least, and perhaps actually impossible. How does the pilot end? I think Ted stomps off the set and out of the building. This can be a ‘Get Smart’ kind of credits clip and we can view it through the lenses of various security cameras. I’m telling you, Reader, the camera issue is just about as vital to the show’s logic as is the ongoing ambiguity of Ted’s fellow actors.

I seem to come up with no end of episode ideas for ‘TVeality’. Ted always plays along for the first half or so of each show before losing it again in exasperation. One time one of Ted’s fellow actors falls and breaks his arm and Ted eventually makes a big deal about it being fake and how he’ll be perfectly healed in the next episode—and then Ted falls and breaks his own arm and is trying to explain to whoever will listen that it is a genuine break, not just acting (of course he gets medical treatment, just like the first injury victim); but the truly delectable part is that both Ted and the other guy wear casts for the next few episodes. Another time someone on the show dies and there is a funeral for him; of course Ted gets antsy at the funeral and just has to point out that the casket actually only contains a dummy and the real story is that the actor in question broke his contract with the studio or went into drug rehab or whatever; and you also know, Reader, that by the time Ted really gets worked up and has that corpse out of the coffin trying to make it stand up and act right, you will be seeing a television funeral like none you’ve ever seen before. (I leave it to the discretion of the director, Ted’s boss, whether or not the deceased actor reappears in his regular role in future episodes or not). Yet another time there is someone making a guest appearance on the show, but the problem (for Ted, if no one else) is that this guest is a cartoon character (my preference is the little Martian from Bugs Bunny); I will leave this episode to your imagination. Anyhow, I think you get the gist, Reader. I could go on and on with my ideas for 'TVeality'. It is such a potent vehicle for an apostate like myself!

Chapter 8

I guess I let LA slip out. I had kind of intended not to. I mean, I did plan quite definitely to share with you some of my experiences there, but I had been toying with the idea of referring to it as Afar City, and to another locale I sampled there in the States as Anotherfar City, and the States itself as Adistantland. Kind of unwieldy, huh? Kind of stupid of me, huh? Yeah, probably. Well, I'm too lazy anyway to be bothered. That, really, is what makes me such a fastidiously honest individual: laziness. Pure laziness (that and conditioning). Spitting out the truth is effort enough for a tightfisted—tightlipped, I mean to say—individual like myself; spinning a pack of lies on top of that is too much work altogether.

LA. I was traveling by then, definitely traveling, no longer camping. My transition from camper to traveler had commenced with the first conversation I had had with Lewretch in Victoria and had been reinforced by the disheartening information received from him in another conversation in Vancouver, but it was only a few days prior to my arrival in LA, when I was on the bus from Acapulco to Tijuana that, as the final step in the process, I cut my last remaining tie to society and became a full-fledged traveler, the island Samuel Martin.

Please allow me to introduce myself, Reader. I am the former Samuel Martin. You can call me Samuel. If you are a Sinaloense or Sonorano then it could even be that you have already heard of me. Samuel Martin, also known as El Zapato. Let me reassure you, though, that in reality I was nothing more than a simple wayfarer doing my best—and all but bending over backwards—to ride that bus to Tijuana without drawing any attention to myself.

It all started in Acapulco. Well, you know it all started considerably earlier than that, but Acapulco will do. Beautiful city. Too many people, just like LA. And it is similarly ruined, but the locale is stunning. A bay ringed by high hills. Blue, blue, translucent water. Fishermen on the beach with dragnets. I saw one guy butchering a ray he had just caught. The sun was north of me when I was there, the only time in my life it has been that.

I wanted to stay in Acapulco. An elegant lady with silver hair offered me a tutoring position at a university there. It was mine for the taking and it would have supported me comfortably enough. All I had to do was call home and get someone to arrange an official copy of my transcripts from the University of Calgary to be sent. Not an option, unfortunately. This was particularly galling to me because I think I saw Miss Universe there on the campus and she had a friendly smile and I know, I just know, I would have gotten her into my tutorial class. Long, dark hair; tall, graceful, willowy physique; almond eyes. Had I been able then, as I am now, to go into a Quinko's and come out forty minutes later with five-star—okay, passable—documentation, I would still be down there in Acapulco, conjugating with Miss Universe (or fighting the other inmates for my portion of the rat stew at the local hoosegow after the segment Unresolved Mysteries did on me ran).

So, blame it on Acapulco. Did you know, Reader, that those people don't even know how to pronounce the name of their own city? Every time I would say Acapulco, they would respond, "Acapoolco?" I would be like, "Yeah, Acapulco. You hard of hearing? Or maybe you need a little help with your English or Spanish or whatever. Acapulco. A-ca-pull-co." Of course, I only thought that. I never said it, being too polite and not wanting to draw attention to myself. If they wanted to be ignoramuses, that was their business. They could call their city whatever they wanted, for all I cared.

Acapulco may have had a Quinko's, but I never saw it. So maybe I would've been out of luck anyway. México is funny. In some ways it is just as modern as us. Take their inter-city buses, for instance. The economy coaches put the Greydog to shame, they really do, and the luxury coaches have no similar counterpart north of the Rio Grande, not unless you start including airlines and their business class seating in the comparison. Anyway, whether I was to remain in Acapulco or leave I needed new ID. The flight I'd taken to Puerto Vallarta was set to return and as soon as that occurred, and the man that I was did not return with it, there would be a definite lead for some clever pursuer of mine to recognize.

It was a pity that I had to discard that identity. Will Collins. Being my very first documented improvisation, it had cost me a great deal of time and effort in Vancouver where I had created it. The name had come from the publisher of the Bible my parents had given me as a child, minus the "and sons". I figured I would be able to remember that name since it was so familiar to me. Anyway, although Alberta has converted to the new driver's licenses that look like credit cards, I still had one of the old ones, the two-part with the picture card and an accompanying document. This was good for me because it gave me something to work with. (The new IDs, although presumably easy to acquire illegally within Alberta since the government has privatized their issuing, are otherwise out of my league). My first task in creating that ID had been to obtain an appropriate photo of myself, my new, blond and bespectacled self as of then. This was pretty straightforward: I just went to a passport photo service in downtown Vancouver and got some that way, enough copies to give me scope for a little trial and error. (Since then I have learned always to keep 3 or 4 such photos on me at all times—saves bother and cuts down on delays). Then I had to create the documentation. Being my freshman effort, I was trying to be a little too literal in my copying of genuine ID. What I mean to say is that, unless you are willing to steal someone else's genuine data and insert it all into the ID you are manufacturing, your "government-issued" ID is never going to withstand governmental scrutiny, whether that of police, customs or what-have-you. So why bother aiming for perfection otherwise? Instead of trying to create a literally perfect document flawed by untenable data, why not just aim for a presentable document purportedly from some jurisdiction at the other end of the country (or continent)? This is something I have figured out over the last ten months, but back there in Vancouver I was still learning the ropes.

Once I had my photos I went to a copy shop to make—redo—my documentation. My plan was simply to scan in my valid ID and make the obvious alterations to the data in it. This sounds easy enough, but it really wasn't. First of all, I had never used a scanner before, so I had to get up to speed on that. Secondly, my Alberta documentation had not been developed in any Microsoft kind of format, plus it had print elements that did not transfer well from paper to screen. And thirdly, what with juggling between text and graphics and working with questionable fonts and positioning and a bunch of other annoyances, I kept getting bogged down and having to beg for help from the pretty girl with a heavy Russian accent who was running the place. What I had thought would be a 15-minute task extended well past an hour—and doing something of questionable legality like that left me increasingly nervous as time slid past. Initially when I had tapped Svetlana for advice I had been fairly discreet and had just asked her how to do this or that rather than getting her to show me. Later on, as my frustration and desperation mounted, I became less and less cautious until finally, by the end, I just threw discretion entirely to the wind and got her to help me finish the cursed thing and get it printed out. I had vaguely hoped that her being from another culture and English being her second language would keep her from recognizing that I was busily forging documentation there in her shop. As if! Ludmila was a very kind girl and a good judge of character, but she wasn't entirely blind to the glaringly obvious. At the point where finally she just had to stay standing behind me telling me exactly what to do, step-by-step and key-by-key, she smiled with a little roll of her eyes and—bless her heart!—said, "Whatever it is you are doing, I am looking the other way". Man, I love an accent!

Reader, I am sure you are thinking that after that copy shop ordeal I deserved an easy completion of my new driver's license. This really should have been the case. All that was left to do was to laminate the photo card. How tough could that have been, questionable legality and all? As a matter of fact, it's not tough at all, as I have since discovered. Most Quinko's have a laminating service and their workers are not so well paid that you won't find one who will do your laminating for you right then under your watchful eye for a $10 or $20 tip. You just need to be discreet in your approach and be willing to walk out the door sans $10 if there is any funny business. But I had yet to learn all that. After cutting my photo card and passport photo into the right size and shape (I suggest you always use a razor, not scissors, for this operation), I went to an office supply store and tried out their laminating machine, a floor display model. Laugh all you want, Reader, but this actually was a good idea and would have worked out perfectly, except for the fact that the photo in my ID created too much of a bulge in that spot and jammed the machine. Was I ever glad I had back-up copies to work with because in pulling my ID back out of the machine I tore it in half (and ended up leaving part of it stuck in the stupid thing). That left me with Plan B: yon Narmy and Avy store down on skid row. They sold clothes irons. A laminating machine is just a heater, you know? Clothes iron, laminating machine: same difference, right? They both get things hot and flat. So I toddled down to Narmy and Avy. At this point I must just have looked suspicious because I had hardly gotten into the store when I picked up a tail from security. What a headache! Had OfficeManx called over here with a laminating alert APB or what? Did this guy really think that I, Nicholas Porter (since I was still a few minutes shy of assuming my Bible name), would ever stoop to shop-lifting? And particularly in Narmy and Avy? Puuuh-lease! It was not as if the clothes iron was going to be going anywhere. All I wanted was to use it—test it out, for heaven's sake—for about two minutes and I promise I'll put it right back in its box (after letting it cool down) and put the box back on the shelf with all the rest. Man, oh man, people! Cut me just a little slack here!

Well, eventually my shadow in Narmy and Avy got tired of my patient browsing and went looking for greener pastures. So I slid over to housewares, picked out my iron, found a plug-in and fired it up. She was a beauty, compact but substantial, and smoking hot. I had my new ID laminated in the blink of an eye, then I skedaddled. A little more razor work a few minutes later, plus some corner-trimming (with nail clippers—that's the only easy way to get corners on ID to come out right) and a little scuffing, and I was a whole new me.

Do you understand now, Reader, why I was rather attached to that identity? I'd put my heart and soul into it—or, at least, a ridiculous amount of effort. All the same, it had to go. The flight out of Puerto Vallarta without me, that me, dictated that. I was fairly familiar with Acapulco by this time. I had gone to the beach a little and I had run around the city a fair bit trying to find a job that would support me yet not involve contact with tourists. And something that I had not seen, and the presence of which would in fact have surprised me there in Acapulco, was a good, full-service copy shop equipped with customer-accessible computers. I say that it would have surprised me partly because it is such a new innovation and partly because everything here in México is just a little closer to the bone than up north. People are poorer. There is more desperation and class alienation. Subsequently, there is far less social trust in the economic sphere. Stores tend to be small with a low ratio of merchandise to merchant so that proprietors are not stretched too thin in watching over their wares like hawks. Even low value items, low-value manufactured items that is, are often kept in display cases so that clerk assistance is necessary for their handling. The value of technology and machines outweighs that of labor here to such a degree that self-service in general not only entirely lacks economic merit to the consumer but also carries with it unacceptable risk to the merchant. You can see, then, why I did not expect to be able to get my hands on a good computer there in Acapulco for an hour or two of intensive documentation. (Even here in Mazatlán it took me some hard digging and an unorthodox approach—I eventually had to settle for going to a private home—before I was able to access a computer).

So, instead I settled for simply destroying the nice photo-ID I was carrying without replacing it, and altering the accompanying birth certificate. When I had made the birth certificate in Vancouver I had produced it from scratch and I doubt if it took me ten minutes. You can do this, Reader, make a birth certificate or baptism certificate just out of your head, because there are thousands of issuing agencies throughout North America and nobody will ever question or confirm the legitimacy of your document—just pick some defunct issuer a long ways away from where you plan to use the document. Yet, even this pared-down effort of mine was a hassle there in Acapulco. First I had to delete the data off the original I was using (it was a nice original) and of course I couldn't use the photocopier myself, I had to let the lady at the copy shop I had found in the Zocalo do the copying and thus have the opportunity to stick her nose into my business. (I didn't know at the time how well Mexicans mind their own business, so when I came out of that shop I took a little peek around the square for that tightening noose of federales and thought with a shudder about the demise of Butch Cassidy and the Sundance Kid). Then I had to insert my new data, my Samuel

Martin data—I had chosen that name because it sounded possibly Hispanic (which, for some reason, I thought would be helpful, though I can't remember or understand why now)—into one of the blanks. And do you think I could get my hands on even a typewriter? No, of course not. So I had a few blank birth certificates that I couldn't fill in. (It was bad enough to have to get help making these blanks, but I certainly wasn't letting anyone see the replacement data going into them, one of them.) Eventually I compromised by going to a typing shop and getting one of the girls there to type up some innocuous looking document that I took back to my hotel and chopped apart for the choice tidbits I needed to paste into my birth certificate. And finally it was back to the copy shop for Sundance and one more run of the gauntlet. Whew! No wonder Mexicans need a three-hour siesta by the time mid-day rolls around. If you think being a self-respecting fugitive is all Bolivian Riviera and Margaritaville like in the movies, have I got news for you, Reader. It is hard work. Hard work, long hours and low pay (even no pay, often as not).

I spent too long in Acapulco. I had thought that I was going there to stay. When it truly dawned on me that this would not be happening, my money supply was just enough to get me back to civilization. So I hightailed it back out of there on the bus for Tijuana, and it was this bus-ride, the brief odyssey on the stretch from Mazatlán north, to be precise, which gave rise to the legend of El Zapato.

Traveling in México by bus is a pretty casual, enjoyable affair. The scenery is beautiful: verdant and mountainous in Guerrero; hilly or mountainous everywhere else in the interior; dry and deserty in the north; and the starkest, ruggedest moonscape you could ever imagine traversing the spine of Baja (except for the discordant horse pastures at the very top). Every now and then—emphasis on every—the bus stops and you get to check out some dusty little town or larger city. Along with el baño (el banyo, not el bane-o, though usually that is true enough), usually designated for caballeros and damas (and you are one or the other whether you have ever ridden a horse or not, Reader), amenities inevitably include tortillas and tamales. A lot of people—certainly all tourists—will urge you to steer very clear of food prepared like this in a cart on the street (or, in the case of tamales, sold out of some old sack they're carried around in). You know, you be your own judge there. I tried for a few days straight in Acapulco to accustom my body to the tap water, and I finally got tired of running—running—for a pitstop and so I now drink only bottled water in México; but I eat street vendor food on occasion and I haven't seemed to have run into any problems doing so.

Bus travel being so laidback like this here, you can see that I was really enjoying the trip north from Acapulco. First I bought a fare to México City and, once there, I got one for Tijuana. I even practiced my Mexican accent on the ticket girl in México City by replying, "Hernando Cortez," to her when she asked, "¿Nombre?" And I swear she didn't bat an eye as she typed Hernando Cortez onto my ticket. So I was feeling good as the bus brought me nearer and nearer to somewhere where I could get work and survive. I was feeling good, that is, until Mazatlán and my first border-check, like, totally out of the blue.

Border-check?! Did I really mean to write that? Yes, Reader, I said, "Border-check". Five hundred miles from their nearest border and these jokers want to interrupt my vacation just so they can shake me and my fellow travelers down. Where is Cesar Chávez when you need him? Or Emilio Zapata? Or Che Guevara? All I ask for is a little social justice. I really don't need all this heat. Don't these federales have speeders they should be pursuing? Or people parked illegally? Or stop-sign runners? There are a million traffic violators out there and these creeps want to waste their time pestering a quiet and unprepossessing fugitive from the law like myself. If I had any money to grease their palms with, do you think I'd be riding the Greydog? Come on, gente! Use your heads a little!

So I'm seated three quarters to the back of the bus on the driver's side when Pancho Villa steps on and I feel the instant tension of my fellow riders. He starts checking IDs and tickets person by person as he makes his way toward the back. What on earth is going on here? It's not supposed to be like this! I'm still carrying my gold card, my Gary Wilson gold card from American Excess! Sure, I knew I had to let that baby go before hitting the border at Tijuana. I fully intended to. But ambushing me like this a ten-day burro ride from la línea? This is just plain dirty pool, the dirtiest pool I've ever seen. Never, ever, ever has Hollywood so much as breathed a word about this particular little nasty trick. Getting across the border into Old México might be a struggle, but once you're there it's smooth sailing. That's the way it's supposed to be!

I'm sweating buckets by this time. The guy in the mirror shades is getting closer and he really seems to be hassling people. Of course, I don't know exactly what's going on because they aren't even trying to speak in English. A couple seats ahead of me the federale finds a young man he really doesn't like. After harassing him on the bus for a couple minutes he makes him grab his bag out of the overhead bin and get off the bus. I don't know what the kid did or said, but they shook him down good out there and he never did get back on the bus. Once Pancho was done with that he got back on the bus himself to finish his predations. Finally he got to me. I hid my nervousness the best I could (which probably wasn't all that good). To his first question, which was something along the lines of, "¿!¿!¿!¿!¿!¿!¿!¿!¿!¿!¿!!!????????" I replied, "My ticket? Oh, here it is." And I produced it for him. He seemed cool with that. Then, to his second question, which was basically, "¿!¿!¿!¿!¿!¿!¿!¿!¿!¿!¿!!!????????" I followed up with, "Oh, I bought the ticket in México City. I'm traveling to Tijuana, and from there to Los Angeles." He seemed a little dissatisfied with that response, and I can't say that I blamed him because I had a sneaking hunch he really had been asking about ID. The problem on my part with entertaining questions vis-a-vis ID was that, as you well know, Reader, I had none worth mentioning, so I felt it was best just to keep off the subject. Now, if I had been talking to myself, this strategy would have worked out okay; but I wasn't, I was talking to an underpaid Latin American policía who had the time, energy and interest to persist in his interrogation of myself. To his third and tenacious-sounding, "¿!¿!¿!¿!¿!¿!¿!¿!¿!¿!¿!!!????????" I was like, "Oh! You want my luggage receipt!" And my face looked like a lightbulb that had just been flicked on. Enlightenment! So I made a huge production of digging in my pocket and locating the little stub with which I would be claiming my bag in Tijuana. "There you go, Officer. Yes, I do have luggage in the storage bin beneath the coach. One bag. Just one bag. Uno. Uuuu-no."

By this time my fellow travelers were getting fairly curious. Pancho Villa had been pestering everyone, but his advance had quite obviously bogged down with me.—Which was the very last thing I wanted! Heat! Maybe México was a little behind the times, a little out of the loop, but my unused return flight to Vancouver meant that there was a definite possibility the authorities here had been put on alert to watch for and arrest me. Anyway, after playing dumb to a couple more of Pancho's questions I finally gave in and said, "Oh! Documentos!" Like, I get it now! But, really, on the inside I was like, "Okay, you little creep! You want to see my papers? You're going to see it, not them, it! And I hope you enjoy looking over this piece of crap because that's all it is! A piece of crap, a photocopied piece of crap!" So I commenced to untie my right shoe and retrieve my folded up birth certificate, my proof of Samuel Martin-ness. (I kept it in a plastic bag under my foot in my shoe because I really did not want to lose it or have it stolen from me like the rest of my ID, you know? Officer?)

You would have thought that Pancho had never seen someone carrying his birth certificate in his shoe before, Reader. He looked at me like I was off some other planet. He didn't know whether to laugh or become enraged. I tried to hand him the birth certificate after I had carefully unfolded it out flattish, but he had to act like it carried leprosy or something and instead had me hold it up for him to look it over. I thought he was overdoing it just a little. I mean, I did keep the thing sheathed in plastic. It wasn't like it was soggy with sweat or particularly smelled—though I admit that it was a little humid and droopy. And where were we anyway? México! Like, hello?! I'm not saying the place is a cesspool—and I love it and the people here, I really do—but it's not as if the hygiene standards down here are anything remotely equivalent to what they are up north.

I don't know if Pancho finally twigged on to the fact that no income supplement would be forthcoming from myself, or if he decided it would be beneath his dignity to accept monetary assistance from someone like myself, or if maybe even he was just fairly scientific in his shakedown actions and had a five-minute ceiling on encounters. I really don't know, but I do know that my birth certificate left him entirely unimpressed. At any rate he just basically threw up his hands and continued on after having looked the thing over and shaking his head in derisive dissatisfaction. I wasn't sure if the interview was over or if he was coming back, so I didn't put it back in its hiding place till he had gotten off the bus and we had pulled out of the bus station.

I don't know how long this entire crisis lasted, start to finish, Reader. Fifteen, twenty minutes. Yet it's amazing what a rich and varied thought life you can have in a mere twenty minutes or so. In my mind's eye I had seen hurried phone calls to headquarters and foreign embassies, maybe even the RCMP or the FBI. I had seen quick-witted underlings recalling a recent APB about a Canadian wanted in connection with some kind of mystery down in Texas. I had seen staff meetings in which federales were told to be on the look-out for said Canadian as he had been tracked to Puerto Vallarta (just a couple hours to the south) where the trail had gone cold. I had had visions of Mexican prisons full of Mexican desperadoes and Mexican drug-smugglers—plus one Canadian traveler with an ambiguously English name. I'd seen all these things and many more besides, all in a matter of minutes, nightmare bursts punctuated by sights of the tangible threat inspiring them.

Despite my richly nightmarish thought life, as the bus pulled out of Mazatlán the thing that most filled my mind was my gold card. It wasn't mere vanity that had caused me to keep it up to that point. I had kept it for one reason and one reason only: dire emergency. Having cut all other ties to society (and I most definitely had, Reader), I was entirely on my own. I depended entirely on myself—with this one exception that were I to fall deathly ill or be seriously injured in some way I would throw this elixir at the problem and be guaranteed adequate medical assistance, even though such would be followed inevitably (and likely immediately) by my apprehension. As I stated earlier, I had in fact already decided to dispose of this card prior to re-entering civilization, so it's not as if it took any soul-searching there on the bus. Nevertheless, it was a momentous act, pulling the card out of my wallet (where I'd had it tucked inside an innocuous looking paper) and bending it back and forth till it broke. If sequestration had been my first step on my way to islandhood, and my acceptance of a fugitive existence my second, this sundering of my one remaining tie—the destruction of my Get-Into-Jail-Free card—was the last. I had become an island.

I hadn't wasted any time destroying my gold card after leaving Mazatlán, and it was a good thing. At the very next stop—Obregón? Does that sound right?—it was the exact same routine all over again. You know where I'm seated: tucked away fairly out of sight yet with a view of the entrance. It's Pancho's prima this time, but otherwise his exact replica. She starts checking IDs and tickets person by person as she makes her way toward the back. I am so glad, so glad, that I've disposed of my gold card. (I got rid of the pieces in el baño moments before). Prima is getting closer and she really seems to be hassling people. However, unlike Pancho, she still has an unsated appetite. Finally she gets to me. I am quite nervous, but hide my nervousness the best I can (which probably wasn't all that good). To Prima's first question, which is along the lines of, "¿!¿!¿!¿!¿!¿!¿!¿!¿!¿!!!????????" I reply, "My ticket? Oh, here it is". And I produce it for her. So far, so good. She seemed cool with that. Then, to her second question, which was basically, "¿!¿!¿!¿!¿!¿!¿!¿!¿!¿!!!????????" I follow up with, "Oh, I bought the ticket in México City. I'm traveling to Tijuana, and from there to Los Angeles". She seemed a little dissatisfied with that response, and I can't say I blamed her because I had a sneaking hunch that she really had been asking about ID. The slight twitter from the other passengers surrounding me in the bus didn't help matters, I'm sure. To her third and tenacious-sounding, "¿!¿!¿!¿!¿!¿!¿!¿!¿!¿!!!????????" I am like, "Oh! You want my luggage receipt!" And my face looks like a lightbulb that has just been flicked on. Enlightenment!—Oh, would you people please shut your mirthful yaps?! Please! It's me, your fellow traveler talking here. It is not you I am performing for, and your enthusiastic expressions of amusement are not appreciated at this time! Thank you!—Making a huge production of digging in my pocket, I locate the little stub with which I would be claiming my bag in Tijuana. "There you go, Madame Officer. Yes, I do have luggage in the storage bin beneath the coach. One bag. Just one bag. Uno. Uuuu-no".—And would you believe these cursed people, Reader? Not only are the whole bunch of them outright cackling at this point, but a couple of them have the nerve to chant Uuuu-no with me when they hear it coming the second and more emphatic time.

Well what is a guy to do at times like this, Reader? An island, that is. Clam up? Have a nervous breakdown? This reminds me of a time ten or twelve years ago when Sep and I were selling merchandise door-to-door one summer. Really, Sep was selling and I was little more use than a pack mule, but a reliable and necessary pack mule all the same (besides which, I did provide the capital). We were talking to this couple at the front door and Sep had them close to buying a couple items, a $20 or $30 sale. All of a sudden, standing there and being supportive yet trying not to interrupt at all, I look at the packaging on a set of kitchen knives I'm holding and I see some amusing spelling mistake on it. I can't even remember what was spelled wrong. It's not as if that's any big deal because the English on cheap consumer goods produced in the Far East is often awkward. However, that slight amusement combined with the intense need right then for seriousness on my part put me into quite a state. Poor Sep! He had been within a hair of closing the sale when from behind him I start chirping uncontrollably in my efforts to suppress my giggles. He continued to forge ahead with his marketing effort to the people, but it was no use. They kept looking from the merchandise they had been about to buy to me with a Hmmm on their faces like I knew something about the crap that they didn't.—Yet I don't! I'm laughing at this crappy Rustomatic Brand kitchen knife set I'm holding here, people, not the Shrapnelix Brand crap bakeware set or the Shardolite Brand crap crystal set you are considering purchasing. Let the Sepster make his sale!—So anyway, back to Prima and the other passengers on the bus. I knew exactly how Sep had felt that day in Bonneville trying to make a successful presentation to that couple as I sat there looking at Prima and trying to present to her the simple facts of the matter while having my feet kicked out from under me by the peanut gallery.

Like I said, what is a guy to do? What else, but forge ahead? So Prima got a couple stonewalls to her next questions and then, when she persisted, I gave her the, "Oh! Documentos!" routine. Oh, the pinhead gallery loved this! It was better than Mexican TV. They knew just what was coming next. ¡El Zapato! ¡El Zapato! Tee-hee-hee-hee-hee! I felt like Ted in 'TVeality' must feel at the point in the show, in each episode, when he can't take it anymore and just loses it, dashing the mask to the ground. However, I did continue with the role. Who knows? Maybe the one person still in a state of suspended disbelief was the only person who mattered, the only person for whom I was actually performing. Untying my right shoe, I retrieved my birth certificate, unfolded it out flattish and drooped it up over my left hand for Prima to look it over. Reader, you would have thought that Prima had never seen someone carrying his birth certificate in his shoe before. She looked at me like I was off some other planet. She didn't know whether to laugh or scream at me. After looking from me to it and back to me again (and thinking nasty thoughts I'm sure), she wrinkled her nose—which was completely unnecessary—and fixed her eye on the birth certificate for a thorough inspection. At this point the bus went dead silent. I don't know if the other passengers were cheering for a thumbs-up or a thumbs-down, but they sure were holding their breath—as was I—awaiting the outcome. Finally, with a sigh of resignation and a roll of her eyes, Prima moved on. Not another word to me. I didn't know if the interview was complete or if she might be coming back, so I didn't put my birth certificate away again till she had gotten off the bus and we had pulled out of the station.

Reader, did you happen to notice the parallels between these two ordeals, the one with Pancho Villa and the other with Prima? I could keep on like this, looking back over what I have written and copying it over and over for each such encounter between there and Tijuana, they were all so much the same. My fellow travelers played their role each and every time. They never seemed to tire of my misfortunes. (Truth to tell, they were probably keyed up the whole time with that ever-present fear, each of them, of being the one who would get jacked, so that their schadenfreude was more an expression of relief than the result of ennui). Their performances waxed and waned (mostly waxed) from stop to stop, but they remained consistently annoying and nerve-wracking for me throughout. And how many more stops did we make, how many more border-checks did we have, before getting to Tijuana and the actual border? Six more! Eight in total, count them. One, two, three, four, five, six, seven, eight! And the only one where the federales eased off and just stopped the bus cursorily was the one I had been dreading the most, the final one after we had come over the spine of Baja and were approaching Tijuana.—Which was so anti-climactic after the build-up to it provided by the previous seven that I very nearly stormed to the front of the bus to lodge my protest at such neglect!

So there you have it, Reader: the true misadventures of El Zapato. How's that for a baptism by fire? You are now a full-fledged island, 100% pure. Still think it's all it's cracked up to be? Still yearning to break out of suburbia and live an intensity-filled life?

Chapter 9

Imagine a dog's-eye view documentary of daily life in Mazatlán. Walking along the sidewalks downtown. Old Mazatlán is not like a North American city at all. Mediterranean, I think. Very pre-Frank Lloyd Wright. Definitely not formatted with the motor vehicle in mind. There is a rundown and abandoned old status building on Belisario or Dominguez whose nameplate identifies it as the British embassy; and as imposing and stately as this three-storey structure is, it has this tiny, skinny little garage door imposed on it by modernity, just an unimposing little crack in its structure for a Silver Cloud or two to ease in and out of. Up north we have streets, mostly two-way, parked cars, boulevards, sidewalks, fences or hedges, front yards, detached homes, backyards, back fences and then alleys, in that exact order and with really only the boulevards as optional. Here in Mazatlán you have streets, mostly one-way (I'm talking about Old Mazatlán), sidewalks and then homes which are independent edifices yet nonetheless butted up tight against the adjacent homes on both sides and behind. Compare these two layouts: five or six extra degrees of civil engineering separation up north and we wonder why we are beset with feelings of alienation.

So walking around Mazatlán is a far more intense experience than walking around your neighborhood back home. The sidewalks are full of people and I've already told you that this city is beautiful-girl-central. Always a mini-skirt swishing by. Always. Then you've got the street filled with cars and buses but everyone poking along fairly slowly because of the traffic lights at every block. The buses hug the curb even tighter here than up north, but that's no big deal. The one genuinely negative thing is the air pollution, the exhaust fumes, but that's only really bad on the main thoroughfares that are a few lanes worth of emissions. Most of the roads are so narrow that they support only a couple lanes. I still don't know where everyone parks.

On the other side of the sidewalk you have the homes, but more often than not downtown these are businesses: shops or what-have-you. Where they are homes these structures might have a couple tall, narrow barred windows and a door as the sole entrance (except for maybe jumping off the rooftop or stepping from one rooftop to an adjacent one). The roof—it's a flat roof with a parapet—is a part of the home here in the same way that our backyards are. There are stairs and a door for easy access. People dry their clothes on lines up there; they send their kids and pets out there to play or bark; and they relax out there in patio chairs just like we do in our backyards. You don't get a sense of this when you are just out walking, although now and then you might see someone looking over a parapet. It was only because I lived in a hotel downtown and was thus able to see all this hidden life from above that I became aware of this aspect of the Mediterranean town.

Their parks are different, too. You might not even call their plazas parks, but it's all the same difference. Except that they are many more times as charming and inviting as our parks are. I don't mean this as a slur on our society. I really, truly love us and that is where my loyalties will always lie. Yet at the same time I have developed a genuine respect and affection for them and I recognize that there are aspects of their society that are superior to our way of doing things and I think we would be wise to learn from them. Anyway, their plazas are these charming little postage stamps used by everyone for everything all at once. If they have any lawns they are tiny, boulevard-like strips. There are always trees; and usually shrubs and flower gardens, too. Otherwise we are talking about hard surfaces, whether cement, cobblestone or pavement. And of course there are lots of benches. The year-round sunny climate allows these plazas to be integrated far more fully into life here than could ever be the case up north, but it's not just the weather—it's the outlook on life here, too. The elderly sit in the sun and chat or read. Families have picnics. Businessmen negotiate. Lovebirds frolic. Office workers relax. Children play, loudly and boisterously. Fruit vendors sell chopped green mangoes doused in sugar and chili powder, or coconuts that they have just hacked open with machetes (at apparent risk to life and limb), or whatever other fruit may be in season. Do you get what I'm getting at, Reader? The Mediterranean plaza is not the specialized or compartmentalized facility that we have allowed our parks to evolve into. It is a togetherness place. Rather than emphasizing differences, whether of age, ability or activity preference, it imposes a commonality of shared experiences on everyone. The Mediterranean plaza takes neighbors and transforms them into family, extended family.

I hope I've given you an idea of what it is like merely to wander around Mazatlán on foot. There is one other macro-aspect that I need to describe to insure that we are entirely on the same wavelength. This is a paradigm difference and it affects everything. What I am talking about is personal responsibility. Not the idealized, Marlboro Man kind of personal responsibility we delude ourselves with up north, but rather a practical, day-to-day, survival-of-the-fittest kind of personal responsibility. One day I was walking down a street and I noticed a bit of rubble on the sidewalk ahead of me. I thought nothing of it, but then I heard voices overhead. These construction workers were hard at work a couple floors up beating apart a wall they were going to replace! No warning signs below. No fenced-off area to detour pedestrians out of harm's way. Nothing. Just a bit of rubble as an inadvertent warning to the watchful. And that was the norm! I eventually came to understand the fundamental difference here: whereas up north we have all but obliterated the concept of inherent hazard, here in México it is still (and quite necessarily) fully understood so that it is the individual who is ultimately responsible for the individual and not society as a whole. There are pros and cons to all this and we are undeniably the stronger, more powerful society—so that is a significant argument for our approach. All the same, the individual who remains cognizant of the inherent hazards in life and approaches it accordingly is the hardier for it. One truly splendid result of this is the wonderful posture you will see in everyone here, and I mean physical posture. No slovenly slouching along like we see all too often up north. Here it's back straight and head up while walking so as to be alert to possible danger on every side as well as above and below. You think I'm joking or exaggerating, Reader? No, I'm not. The posture here is superb. Every Mazatleca, even the least attractive, looks like she'd own any catwalk she might happen to saunter down.

Or let me illustrate this personal responsibility from another angle: One day I was sitting in a plaza and I saw a little girl, maybe seven or eight years old, standing at the edge of the roof of a sunken building and taunting her mother who was standing six or seven feet below on the cement walkway. It was all in Spanish but some things are universal. The little girl was poised up there threatening to jump down just to get a rise out of her mother. Now, what do you think, Reader, would be your typical soccer-mom response? "Oh, baby, be careful. You could get hurt! Mommy doesn't want her little precious to fall and hurt herself.—And where is your helmet, anyway? You know you mustn't ever play outside without your crash helmet, and gloves, and kneepads, and elbow pads, and first-aid kit!" And is that what this young mother said to her little girl? No, not even close. Like I said, it was in Spanish, so I don't know the exact words, but here's the gist of it: "Come on, then, chicken! You're too chicken to jump! Let's see how stupid you really are! Come on! Jump! Jump!" The little girl hesitated then, seeing that her blackmail wasn't going anywhere; but she must have decided that forward was better than backward out of this mess her mouth had gotten her into and so she jumped. I can still hear the slapping noise her little sandals made as she landed. Like, Ow! The sound alone stung the soles of my own feet. The little girl yiped in pain and hopped from one foot to the other as she massaged each foot in turn, but her mother only laughed at her. And that, in my ever humble opinion, Reader, is a very good mother adept at furthering the holistic, long-term wellbeing of her child.

Let's back up now and recall that this is supposed to be a dog's-eye view of Mazatlán that I'm giving you here. Okay, so I kind of forgot to put everything at ground level. I guess you're going to have to just stop for a minute and re-imagine it all down there... The soiled sidewalks in front of your nose. The feet rushing by, including a generous sprinkling of pretty ankles. The car wheels and bus wheels and their exhaust pipes. The bottoms of doors instead of the window parts. Going up and down curbs. Skirting everywhere where fresh rubble is evident. Negotiating the mayhem in the plazas, and on the streets and sidewalks in general, especially the closer you are to El Mercado. Stopping for a rest, even a nap, anywhere you can curl up without being stepped on, be that in a vacant lot or a plaza, or a quiet stretch of sidewalk on the shady side of the street, or an idle-looking doorway, or wherever.

I've tried to imagine Mazatlán from this perspective. Same city as what I've been seeing, but certainly a very different experience. All of the contrasts with North American city life—the sights, the smells, the sounds—emphasized considerably. For instance, you're never going to get a faceful of exhaust when some old boat chugs by in the curb lane. And I'm sure the clip-clip-clip of a smart set of stilettos strutting by must be ten times as urgent when your ears are six inches off the sidewalk. Anyway, I've been inspired to consider this dog's-eye view of

Mazatlán by the sight of this guy I kept seeing everywhere here. I don't know if he is homeless, but he appears to be; and I don't know if he lives off of charity or scavenging, but he sure doesn't seem to be fit for much else. That said, I really respect the guy. Something was wrong with his back and he could not stand upright, but he didn't let this condition incapacitate him—as it would virtually anyone in a more advanced society like ours. The guy "walked" everywhere on his hands and his feet, all fours; not on his hands and knees, but hands and feet. He was bent right over double and he held his head as high up as he could so as to be looking forward as much as possible rather than downward. Needless to say, Reader, it was one of the strangest things I've ever seen, seeing this guy sawhorse by like that. I pitied him for his condition, yet I also respected him to no end for not letting it get him down—literally, get him down. Whenever I see such determination as that I cannot help but respect an individual.

I feel a special kinship to this sawhorse-man because of my own experience on the streets of LA last summer. No, I had no disability dragging me down, as did he. However, at times, the worst of times, it was nothing but sheer determination that got me by. So I look at this guy, a broken, unwashed wreck of a man, very possibly all but cast out from his society, and in his determination to forge ahead I see, I feel, a brother-in-arms.

Chapter 10

L.A. It would have been a gravy train for a tough old dog like Sawhorse—we are such a fabulously wealthy society, all but swimming in riches. To a recent excommunicant like myself, though, a newborn island whose lava flows had yet to harden and cool, much less erode and allow purchase by a new clothing of life, it was one of the toughest slogs I've ever slogged.

I sailed into Tijuana nearly flat broke. I had hung around Acapulco too long, obviously. Well, that was okay now. I was back in a first world economy. I felt like an illegal alien, though. Between me and the Promised Land was a high fence, a short stretch of no-man's-land and a million or so border patrols. No big deal. I hopped on a city bus headed for the beach planning to swim north along the shore till finding myself in San Diego.—Yes, Reader, I really did plan to do that. I'd heard stories when I took a trip to San Diego once in Grade Twelve about Mexicans jumping in taxis soaking wet out on Coronado Island or Point or whatever and I figured they had to get there somehow. So, if they could swim it, so could I.—Anyway, once I hit the beach in Tijuana and saw that there was a fence built out into the ocean it kind of twigged on me that maybe, just maybe, the Gringos had this angle covered by now.

I spent the rest of that day analyzing my situation and I decided that the best thing to do was just to cross the border like usual. I had already weathered more than half a dozen border checks, after all, so what was one more? Not wanting to look too ragged for this undertaking, I decided to wait till morning and in the meantime find some fleabag motel to get a proper sleep in. And that was no problem whatsoever in Tijuana. (Reader, if you have allowed some border town experience like Tijuana to formulate your perception of México, please do yourself an enormous favor and go further in to where you will find the culture relatively intact and largely unmarred by outside influences).

The next morning I shopped around for a little while and got myself some props, some tourist junk so that I would fit in with the tourist crowd crossing the border. (I didn't have to bother with any Bermuda shorts or flower-print shirts though—not for Tijuana, thankfully). Then I had to kill a little time. I didn't want to hit the border before two-ish. It was while I was thus twiddling my thumbs that I met Randy, this bottom-feeder extraordinaire. He was an American from San Diego and he had some hardluck story about running out of gas there in Tijuana and needing just five bucks or so to get back home.

Reader, I don't know anything about drug fiends. I've never known any personally. So why would it ever occur to me that somebody could be trying to invest time, effort and thought into some penny-ante endeavor to scam a few bucks out of an unwitting rube like myself? Of course I believed Randy when he described his plight to me. Worse yet, as contributing factors to credulity go, I had a sudden interest of my own in helping this fellow in need in that if he were enabled to drive his wreck across the border, then I would have the opportunity to accompany him in that preferred method of border penetration. So I set out with him on a quest for gasoline, which wasn't quite as straightforward as you would think such a simple task should be. For the life of me, I couldn't possibly imagine why the guy at the gas station was so disinclined to allow dear Randy the use of a gas-can for a few minutes, but he had his mind made up and there was no changing it. Accordingly, we scouted around for a couple old water bottles to use as containers. However, once we found these—and we did—Randy himself seemed to run out of gas. I had to get him into the nearest first aid station and get a pitcher of Corona into him before his battery started to revive. While he was thus convalescing it occurred to me that, being so familiar with Tijuana as he obviously was, he might just be able to help me get some better ID than the birth certificate I was carrying around in my shoe.

Man, what a mistake that was! Yes, Randy was knowledgeable in the matter of fake ID acquisition in Tijuana, but there is a world of difference between having a wealth of information and being willing to share such wealth. I really should have realized what I had stepped in the moment I saw his eyes light up in response to my query. In hindsight, I realize that what I thus saw in his eyes was the recognition of new avenues of manipulation opening up to him. By asking about ID I was all but acknowledging my own vulnerability there. This meant to Randy's mind that I needed something he could provide (or at least hold out the carrot of providing). Worse yet, to go along with this carrot that I had given him there was also the stick of him being able to threaten to report me to the authorities, whether in Tijuana or at the border. Oh, he loved it! He was practically rubbing his hands together and hopping from one foot to the other, he was so excited. But I—like, duuuh!—failed to register the obvious there in my avarice for some nice new ID made by seasoned pros.

So friend Randy and I momentarily shelved the gasoline quest and struck deep into the barrio in search of another new me. Although I was glad to have the company there of someone who obviously knew his way around, I was already starting to get a disturbing vibe out of my would-be benefactor. We were ostensibly going to get me some ID, but he kept explaining to me what to say at the border when they asked why I had no ID. There seemed to be a bit of a disconnect there. It was like we were in a three-way conversation and I was the odd man out. The problem with that was that there were only two of us present. If you've ever dealt with drug fiends, Reader, I'm sure this doesn't sound the least bit unfamiliar to you, altered states of consciousness and all that. I never had before, so it took me a little while to realize that I needed an approach to dealing with him that was different from the standard approach we all (most of us, anyway) have for dealing with new acquaintances. I was basically having to shift from an approach of tentative trust to one instead of tentative distrust, or even outright distrust, an approach entirely alien to me.

We made two stops there in the Spanish Bronx. At the first one Randy went up some stairs to an apartment and came back down with a few IDs to show me. These were apparently stolen IDs and the idea was for me to pick one that kind of looked like me. However, seeing as how the selection was meagre and every last one of them was Hispanic, this was entirely pointless. Besides that, I wanted a manufactured ID, not a stolen one. I don't know the penalties for using a manufactured ID, but clearly it is many times as dangerous to involve oneself with a stolen ID. What were the circumstances of its theft? What if the victim had been injured or even killed, or was missing? So I chastised Randy and we proceeded on our way.

The second stop wasn't about ID. Randy just went in to see somebody. I stayed at the entrance of the complex. After only a few minutes Randy came out to beg for some money and I gave him a few bucks. Even as I gave him that money I knew that I had been led on a fool's errand and I would have to cross the border with my lousy, stinking Samuel Martin birth certificate. That annoyed me, and waiting another twenty minutes or half hour for Randy to re-appear (all blitzy-eyed) further annoyed me. So when he did, I just walked back with him to a more familiar part of Tijuana and eased myself cautiously out of his companionship. He talked about the police in Tijuana as I was becoming conversationally remote, vaguely trying to hint about sicking them on me, but I never rose to his bait and so I was eventually able to shake the little creep with no blatant display of ill feeling between us.

Still having an hour to kill at that point, I wandered around Tijuana and looked at the kitsch in the shops before finally making my way to the border crossing. And who do you think I saw in that last ambush of tourist shops before you get to the border? None other than dear Randy. He was hanging around there furtively selling tiny bits of paper with red dots on them (LSD, maybe?), but also kind of keeping an eye out for me. It must have really been bugging him that he'd let a prime sucker out of his clutches with an unextorted twenty or thirty dollars still in play. Upon intercepting me, his first tack was carrot, but I blew him off and just continued walking. Having nothing left to lose, he switched to stick and went straight for the jugular, "You're not going to get across the border if I have a quick chat with the border guards". Now, how do you reply to that, Reader? What he said was only too true, far truer than he realized. (I had had the brains, at least, to tell him (earlier on) that I'd lost my ID rather than that I was a fugitive. Whether or not he had believed that, who's to say?) Anyway, do you go all cringey and weak-kneed? "Oh, Mr. Randy, please, puh-lee-ee-ee-ee-ease DON'T DO THAT! Here's my wallet. Check my pockets too, if you like. I'm giving you every last cent I have!" Like that, Reader? Think that's a successful negotiation? Of course not. Try a stance like that in such a situation and you'll find yourself not only flat broke but instantly employed as well, and in not the choicest of occupations. So in response to Randy's threat, I said—and with a bit of a PeeWee Herman snarl, "Go ahead! I couldn't care less. I'm sure it won't take them more than a phone call or two to confirm my identity."

That took the wind out of Randy's sails. He stopped without saying another word. I ignored him and continued on my way. I didn't look back until I was ascending the pedestrian overpass, but by then he had made himself scarce.

The border itself was another anti-climax, just like the eighth and last "border check" on the descent into Tijuana. I waited maybe twenty or thirty nerve-wracking minutes before reaching the front of the line. The lady in front of me, or two in front of me, had considerable difficulty and was still there when I left. That was just as well—for me, that is. The border guards simply looked at me and waved me on as I tried to undo my shoe and share my soggy birth certificate with them. I was really glad I'd bought the tourist junk; that alone was better documentation in that specific situation than a walletful of Samuel Martin ID would have been.

Chapter 11

Let me try this again.

LA. (I really didn't think it would take a whole chapter just to get to San Ysidro). You want to hear another pretty girl story, Reader? Another pretty girl frustration, that is? I hop on the trolley, or whatever it's called (it's a light rail train), to downtown San Diego. I really love San Diego. It's the most beautiful city in America: stunning setting; room temperature climate year-round (pretty well); good supply of beaches and beach bunnies; plus it's so clean and well-run that you would think you're in a Canadian city. Canada on the Riviera, that's what San Diego is. So I get on this trolley—a wonderful convenience and I would urge you to use it next time you visit Tijuana—and what do I see? I mean, what do I see, but this Spanish princess straight out of Zorro or some Harlequin romance!!! I'm blinded by my mind's eye just thinking of Zoraya like this! The ever-present long, glossy black hair. Enormous brown eyes. Bone structure that would have wilted Michelangelo's heart: such cheekbones and such wrists! Pretty, pretty lips. And very petite, 5' 1" tops. After I came to and struggled to my feet, I nonchalantly eased—okay, lurched—my way over to her and sat down. It took a few minutes of intensive breathing exercises before I was able to draw a full breath without it sounding like a death rattle, but apart from that I put up a pretty suave and debonair front.

Zoraya was a nanny in Oceanside. Her English was good. Women must find lovestruck fools endearing because we instantly hit it off well. We had a nice chat on the trolley and when we got downtown I walked with her to the bus station and stayed with her until she had to get on the bus. She told me about her visit to her sister in México and she showed me some pictures from her trip, including a couple of her in a black bikini. (Words cannot tell, Reader!) In turn, I told her I was a student in law school—which is true, or was until all of this; that I would be staying with friends in LA after spending a couple days in San Diego—which was stretching it, granted; and that I'd call her in a few days and we'd get together for a date—which I really did hope to bring about despite the obstacles.

Can you see how frustrating that was for me, Reader? Stunning girl. A real sweetie. And we connected so naturally. But not only did I have more important things than Zoraya on my plate (things like survival and freedom, for starters), I lacked even the barest of essentials—a telephone, a car—to pursue any kind of relationship with her. Look on me, Reader, and weep. Spare a little sympathy, a little pity at least, for an island.

Because I ended up in LA, I look back on my trek there and say to myself that I was headed there, but in actual fact I was simply headed to southern California. So, upon reaching San Diego, I would have been just as happy to settle in there as to proceed on to LA. Fat chance of that, though. San Diego is one Republican town. I already said how Canadian it seemed. Well, that's great for a citizen in good standing, but no good whatsoever for a traveling man like myself. First I picked up some of the hygiene necessities I'd had to ditch in Tijuana and then I scouted around the town to find some way to fit myself in there. Had I had even a wee bit of monetary cushion I can say that I would have done alright there, but I didn't have even that. There was no two ways about it: I was going to be sleeping on the beach till I got on my feet. Hey, I can live with that—the only problem was San Diego. The creeps had No Camping and No Trespassing signs all over their beaches and they had posted curfews. San Diego! California! Like, what happened to California Dreaming, and All the Leaves are Brown, and A Warm San Francisco Night, and all that? And it wasn't mere signage. A while after dark I went down to a still-smoldering campfire and kind of made myself comfortable for a little snooze, but I hadn't been there half an hour when some old beach bum wandered by and warned me that the beach patrol was just a little north of us and headed in our direction. Needless to say I didn't welcome any such encounter so I got up and spent the rest of the night not sleeping, one way or another. By morning I had decided that I needed a larger pool to lose myself in than San Diego and so I made my way to the I-5.

I don't recall hitchhiking in California other than this one time. In rural areas of Canada and the United States it's a good way to catch a little local color as you're travelling, and it's not generally too difficult to get a ride. You just stand somewhere not too inconvenient for a driver to stop and you try not to look too scuzzy. Then, once you are in their car, you stay awake and offer them as much conversation as they desire because that is your way of repaying their kindness, giving them someone to visit with. Well, California is a whole different ball of wax. Forget Police Academy and Dumb and Dumber where carloads of hot chicks are just fighting over a guy to give him a ride. That's Hollywood. I'm talking about California. Everyone there is so paranoid that they're more likely to roll up their windows and swerve to the left than to pull off to the shoulder and tell you to jump in.

So I'm standing near the entrance to an on-ramp with my thumb out for, like, two hours. A million cars pass me by. I'm pretty sure that hitchhiking is illegal in California, so every time I see a cop car I drop my thumb and try to act casual, the only non-vehicle out there in a sea of smog trying to blend in with his surroundings. (Really good, Gary—or whoever I was at the time. Samuel, I think, a day or so prior to Cary). Anyway, finally this guy in an SUV stops and I get in. He's on his way home to LA, so I won't have to get a second ride. What a relief!

Buddy was about fifty. He looked like he had probably voted for Clinton. He had a bike and a dufflebag in the back and he said he had been mountain biking near Ensenada, south of Tijuana. He seemed a little distracted the whole time but we chatted a lot. I told him I was a student enjoying the summer and basically headed home to Canada (I guess I was a Canadian at the moment), but that I might look up some friends in LA and spend a few days there. He told me that if I was going to stay in LA for a while and I wanted a job, he had an interest in a health club and he could get me work there. This was really useful, but I didn't have any proper training for that and I told him. All he replied was that it wasn't that kind of health club, as if there is any other kind of health club than a health club and I should understand what he was talking about. I left it at that, a little nonplussed.

LA still hadn't recovered from the earthquake and buddy had to make a couple crazy meanders to avoid unrepaired interchanges. I had had in my mind to aim toward the Venice Beach area youth hostel I had stayed briefly at years ago, but when my benefactor started talking on his cellphone about picking up a pizza and then asked me if I'd help him unload his stuff, I was like Hey. Pizza sounded good to me and it was early in the afternoon, so I'd have the rest of the day to figure out what bus to take to the hostel. The funny thing was that, although we made a couple stops—by this time we were out west on Wiltshire or Santa Monica Boulevard, we didn't end up with any pizza. I know what pizza looks like, Reader, and what it smells like. Whatever it was that buddy had been handed by the scuzzball who had slunk out of the garage we had made our second stop at, it surely wasn't a pizza. Next thing you know, we're headed into the underground parking of an apartment building and buddy's asking me to help him get his bike out of the back.

Reader, you can probably see where this is headed because you are likely a little more knowledgeable in the ways of the world than I am—or, at least than I was before spending a few weeks there in Hollywood. West Hollywood! To me, giving someone a ride is simply an act of kindness, and then taking them into your home and giving them a hot meal is being a genuine Samaritan. I can't tell you how many times I saw my Dad drag home some hitchhiker and see that he got a good meal into him before sending him on his way. If it was in the evening, the guy would even end up with a roof over his head for the night (against my Mom's better judgment, and wishes). So I'm just taking buddy there in LA at face value, at what to me is face value. He needs a hand getting his stuff up to his apartment and he's probably going to whip up some Kraft Dinner or something to share with me. I was still a little puzzled about the pizza, but I had pretty much given up on seeing that.

I wasn't creeped out when I was helping buddy get his stuff up to his apartment, but it sure didn't take long once we got there. First thing he did was hit the bedroom. He had seemed distracted before, but when he came out of there he was acting downright odd. Only then did it dawn on me that maybe his pizza had come in powder form. Then, instead of going to the kitchen and working on food, he starts talking about Let's watch a movie. I'm like, Nooo? Hello? How about Let's eat? He heads back to the bedroom and I start rummaging through the fridge. A minute later he's calling me to come see a movie with him. I poke my head in his bedroom and there he is in bed with the TV on. He asks me if I've ever seen Debbie Does Dallas. I'm like Sigh. I'm like Stare off into the distance. I'm like What on earth am I doing here? I did feel threatened by this slimy situation I found myself in there; but, fortunately—very fortunately—for that slimebucket there, I didn't feel directly threatened by him. I went back to the kitchen, took from my knapsack one of the two fresh-picked oranges I had bought that morning at an outdoor market in San Diego and left it on the table (where I noticed a picture book called 'Young Companions' lying), then quietly slipped out the door.

Hello, LA! So nice to be here.

Chapter 12

L.A. The Promised Land. I was finally there. With eight dollars and change in my pocket. Eight dollars and change. An island with no one and nothing to fall back on. No family. No friends. No welfare state. No charity. No nothing. Me, myself and I, with eight bucks and change. As rich a society as LA is, my existence there was a tightrope. The slightest mistake—a brush with the law, failure to find work immediately, a broken bone, sickness, even a lousy infection—and my fragile island paradise could be toast.

It's funny how the mind works. I look back on this time in LA and see images of warm summer nights, brightly lit streets, Santa Monica beach, Pan-Pacific Park, fresh dawns on Melrose, pretty girls out shopping, flirtatious girls coming into an eatery I worked at, a very pretty girl named Marcie I worked with at another job, and a flood of other pleasant things. I have to stop, though, and remind myself what a miserable time I had there in LA, a truly miserable time, perhaps the most miserable few weeks of my entire life. I know this to be true because I remember sitting down at a picnic table at UCLA one night and writing, writing, writing an impromptu journal covering the previous couple weeks. After ten pages or so I stopped to read over what I had set down, and reviewing it from an arm's length perspective like that brought home to me the ghastliness of it all. Shivering through those warm nights—I had no jacket and it took me eight or ten days to buy a used wool sweater. (I was too chicken to steal what I so desperately needed. I'm not saying too moral. Too chicken.) Going the first week entirely without sleep, not so much as a moment's shut-eye. Trudging along boulevards at night because I had nowhere to go, moving, always moving. Going door to door, hitting up business after business for a job, any job, all day long for three or four days straight. Being offered that job I needed ever so badly and then seeing in the eyes of my would-be employer all that it would entail. The same the following day. (If you don't already know it, Reader, West Hollywood is Queersville. Gay Central. I don't want to give you the impression that all homosexuals are sexual predators, but if you are slender with a clean-cut look to you and you ever find yourself in an economically vulnerable position like I was in, believe you me, you are definitely going to see that particular subculture's dirty linen. It ain't all dancing elves and the colors of Benettar. That's Hollywood. I'm talking about West Hollywood, all the West Hollywoods). Finding a quarter on the sidewalk and registering that such a windfall almost doubled my net worth. Greedily wolfing down day-olds that we were about to dispose of at work. Riding the bus—the crazy train—all night long from one end of LA to the other just to get off the streets. (I thought of it as the crazy train because I saw a lot of street people—crazy weirdoes, the homeless—on it at night going end to end, just like I was). Are you beginning to see, Reader, why I describe LA as being so ghastly for me then? But, like I said, the mind is a funny thing and I have to dredge to recall all this, I have to struggle to keep my fond memories of that time, few and far between though they may be, from overwhelming all the others.

Virtual pennilessness, as an island, is a completely different context from having even just a hundred bucks or so in your pocket. That is what made LA so tough for me. Pennilessness coupled with a complete lack of the skill set needed for making it on the streets. It's not the getting by out there that's so difficult; rather, it's the setting aside of your conventional mindset and the taking on of the necessary new one that is so hard—especially done crash-course style like that.

In my experience out there, there were four fundamental issues: security, food, work and accommodations, and generally in that order. Security always was the over-riding issue, and heightened by the fact that not only was I all alone and without recourse to the authorities, but the authorities themselves were part of this whole threat complex arranged (potentially arranged) against me as well. That sounds kind of paranoid, huh? Well, fortunately, the local authorities, wherever, didn't know that they were against me—the right hand not knowing what mischief the left was up to, you know, Reader?—and I was fully aware of this so that, on that front, my strategy was merely to avoid contact. I did that by remaining very clean-cut and presentable at all times, and also by continuing on as the law-abiding citizen that I have always been. I'm sure that a healthy percentage of fugitives are apprehended due to their ongoing illegal activities or illicit lifestyles.

As to security on the criminal front, despite Hollywood's portrayal of America's streets as rampant with murder and mayhem, it's a pretty secure society we live in, Canada most of all, the States too and even México as well. I maybe should be a little more cautious than I am—meaning that eventually foolhardiness will catch up with a guy, but I have hardly ever restricted my peregrinations on this account. I guess one time when I found myself in Watts I made a point of leaving before dusk. On numerous occasions I was slightly apprehensive, these usually at night, and on a very few occasions afraid, but never enough to break into a run. All of this reflects more on our society than on me.

Food: A penniless island can forget about the whole concept of breakfast, lunch and dinner. Obvious as this may be, it is a very difficult mental transformation to make. Even when I had been camping I had tended to have set times throughout the day which were devoted to the consumption of food. Not so in LA. There it was feed when the feeding was good (with available being the sole criterion of good). Moreover, I had to suspend my predisposition toward good nutrition entirely for the first couple weeks there. Calories, my body was screaming for calories above all else. I found I could go to a dollar store and pick up a pack of cookies containing around 2000 calories, one whole day's worth (though I was probably actually burning around 3000 a day right then) for a lousy buck. Ever think you could survive on $30 a month for food, Reader? I'm not sure you'd want to do so for very long, though. Processed food is bad enough for your system, but limiting it to strictly one form like that must be exponentially worse.

Dollar store cookies may have been my staple for a couple weeks, but I did have other food sources. I bought a lot of over-ripe fruit at the farmer's market. I already mentioned that I ate all the day-old stuff I discreetly could at work. (I started that job about a week after I got to LA). Never did I seek or accept institutional charity, but on two occasions I did accept personal charity. On the first of these I was just chatting with a lady who was on her lunch break when she whipped out a fancy sandwich and insisted on splitting it with me. My pride makes me hope that I didn't look like I needed that act of kindness, but I can hardly begin to say how hungry I was right then, that being maybe my fourth day in LA. The other time I was getting a little rest in a park one afternoon—I had been in LA a couple weeks by then and had found that catnaps in the sun were the most viable source of sleep sans lodging—when another kind lady gave me a couple doughnuts. Once I developed an income, food quickly became almost a non-issue. I took a multi-vitamin, for obvious reasons. I stuck with things like processed food and fruit that didn't need preparation; however, I graduated to a better and better variety of food. My biggest change, though, was the inclusion of a burger for protein each day. I could get the 99-cent special, which was a loss leader, and nothing else, at places like Hack in the Box and Burger Bing. I also drank a lot of milk. (And speaking of drinking, water was definitely an issue. I always carried a plastic pop bottle or two with me and kept them full with fresh water, often even just dumping them and refilling them).

I had a very interesting experience with water, or the lack of it, in late August. I wanted to go to a concert up at Big Bear. There is a bus that goes there, but I didn't know about it until my return trip. So I set out the day before from LA. My plan was to get as close as the public transit would take me and then walk the rest of the way. I hadn't the slightest intention of trying to thumb a ride because it was twilight when I got to San Bernardino and the last stop. I walked for a little while up the highway so as to put the city behind me, then I found a comfortable sand-dune to nestle in. That was the best sleep I had in my whole time in LA. It was quiet. The air was clean. The temperature was pleasant all night long.

When I got up the next morning I began my trudge up the road to Big Bear. It was up, up, up all the way. I really was tempted to stick out my thumb and save myself the walk, but when I thought about what might pick me up I just got disgusted and kept walking. Remember what I said about the spine of Baja, Reader? What a moonscape it is? Well, where I now found myself was basically the northern extension of that. A couple or so miles up and it was just barren rock everywhere, hardly a sign of life to be seen. The highway wound up a canyon with rock walls on one side and rock falls on the other, and I wound with it.

By mid-morning it was beginning to be hot. I had drunk all I had left with me when I woke up. We really take water for granted. You have to be in a situation like this to truly comprehend its value and to understand what a thirsty business traveling must often have been for our ancestors. I kept walking. I began to wonder how far I had to go. The sun was beating down on me fiercer and fiercer as it climbed higher into the sky and reflected off all the rock around me. I don't think that, in reality, I was in any serious danger of dehydration on that little expedition—but I'll tell you, it sure felt like I was. As noon approached I was in agony. I was so thirsty! I began to wonder not only how far I had to go, but how far I had come. Would I be better off continuing on and up, or would I get relief sooner by retracing my steps? I had really wanted to get to the concert—like, obviously—but that was fast becoming of peripheral importance to the scorching heat. And with the swoosh of every passing car I was bitterly impressed with the irony that there went some cool AC and a fifteen- or twenty-minute ride to some sort of fresh water spring, albeit man-made, both available for the asking—the begging on hands and knees, if necessary. Available generally, perhaps, but not available to me, an island.

About the time when I was beginning to wonder if I could take another step I spied, with my little eye, a half-full pop bottle puffed up almost to the point of bursting open. It was a big bottle, a two-liter one, and it was just lying on the shoulder of the road where someone had heaved it from their car. Now, I know exactly what you are thinking, Reader. "Ew! Ugh! Yuck!" —Me too! I am thinking that now and I was thinking that then, even as I was looking it over with lascivious eyes. An entire life's worth of conditioning told me not to touch the dirty thing—its provenance was completely unknown and this was California!—and so it took me three shakes of a lamb's tail, and not just two, to crack it open and suck back the entire contents in a single, uninterrupted swig. That really surprised me. I mean, from the moment I saw the bottle to the moment I extracted my tongue from its neck (where a couple last drops had sought refuge in vain), I was in this trance-like state watching the primeval animal within me kick aside millennia upon millennia of acculturation and civilization so as to seize this life-giving nectar of the gods. First I had looked at the bottle, and sneered. Then I had approached it, and sneered. Then I had picked it up, and sneered. Then I had taken a small sip to ease my thirst—I would throw the rest away—and I was rolling my eyes (at myself) instead of sneering. Then, when I was done taking that little sip, there was nothing left but those couple recalcitrant drops lodged in the neck. That, Reader, was the quickest liter ever in my life. And do you know what? I was still thirsty, really, really thirsty.

Chapter 13

So I wanted to go to a concert up at Big Bear. That must have sounded really discordant to you, Reader, what with the hand-to-mouth existence I was leading at the time. Well, the prospect of listening pleasure wasn't what motivated me to undertake that particular jaunt. I actually had a very serious reason for wanting to attend this concert: ultimately, it was that I wanted—and want—to turn myself in and clear my name. More specifically, it was that I anticipated running into a certain person there at the concert who could have been instrumental in helping me convert the patented technology that I presently own into the money that I will soon need for an adequate defense lawyer. I don't know much about the law and standing trial, but I know this much for sure: All that equal justice under law talk is pure Hollywood, the purest of Hollywood. If I want a fair trial—and I do—then the only way I'm ever going to get it is to pay for it, and pay through the nose. The problem with that is my current state of pennilessness.

Prior to my tangle with the law I had two assets. The first was a gift shop in Houston. I had been in possession of this business only a few months, and so when I disappeared its doors closed fairly immediately. My other asset was this technology I have been working on for the past six years. I was awarded a patent on it a couple years ago now, and this patent is very useful as to giving the technology substance, demonstrating that it's not just some outlandish idea in my head. That said, the value of my patented technology, having yet to make the leap to marketed technology, is entirely intangible. This doesn't mean that it has no value. It just means that its value is an unknown quantity and that very, very few people are capable of making even a ballpark assessment of such value. I had been in touch with one such person, though, over the period of time just prior to my setting out traveling, and it was this individual whom I hoped to track down at the concert up at Big Bear, a concert I knew he was involved with. So, you see, Reader, it wasn't pleasure-seeking, after all, that led me on that wild goose chase. And a wild goose chase it was, because—stupid me!—once I got there and really thought through the risks of identifying myself to this guy and trying to convince him either to buy my patent outright or to finance and otherwise assist me in bringing the technology to market (prior to turning myself in), I realized how very unlikely it would have been that I would have met with a positive outcome.

That may have sounded funny to you, Reader, that I would have thought, even for a moment, that I could convince someone to invest in a high-risk business start-up being managed by a wanted fugitive, and worse yet, that I could have believed this to the extent of planning and undertaking a difficult—for me—expedition toward such an end. Yet, on one level, I really did believe so. They say that people typically use only 5 or 10% of their brain potential. The same is true concerning risk: the average person in our society leads a virtually risk-free life, being exposed on a day-to-day basis to probably well under 5% of the risk that he has the overall capacity to cope with. When I set out to find this guy at that concert, I had been living for the previous couple months at such an elevated risk level, maybe 30 or 40% of capacity, that to me risk had become commonplace and routine, and the avoidance of it ludicrous. I forgot to put myself in that guy's shoes and see that the risk, even if outweighed by the potential reward, was simply unthinkable. It really didn't matter how great the pay-off might have been in the end, or that the actual risk was well within anyone's capacity to cope with, this risk was still way beyond that level which people in our society are conditioned to accept. I lost sight of that and it took me a trip up to Big Bear where I finally had to confront the full array of possible and likely responses I would get from this guy before it became clear—and obvious—to me again.

Experience is an interesting thing, Reader. I just gave you a perfect example of the importance and value of experience. You can look into the future and make all kinds of big (or little) plans and you can tell yourself, “I will do this and this,” or you can think concerning yourself, “I would do this,” or, “I would not do such-and-such, not I”. But until you have actually been in a situation, I guarantee you, Reader, that you do not fully understand all the factors pertinent to it, including yourself and your own capacities, tolerances and responses. I will tell you this, and I promise it’s true: You are far braver than you think yourself to be (unless you are on testosterone overload, in which case you are already familiar with your upper limits and you need to understand that in certain situations you are going to surprise yourself with some genuinely unexpected cowardliness). The same is true regarding all sorts of character qualities, though I don’t mean to say you are consistently better than you expect yourself to be. In some ways you will exceed your expectations and in others you will disappoint them. However, the higher you set your expectations, and the stricter you are about choosing your role models, the better your performance will be. And in the end, it is only experience, the actual situation each time, which demands your full grasp of reality. The more intense the experience, the more fully you will encounter reality, including that part of reality which is composed of yourself.

Chapter 14

I had some really interesting and intense experiences kayaking out on the west coast, along Vancouver Island, to be precise. I kayaked a lot at summer camp when I was a kid, and later a counselor, so I am familiar with the sport on a casual level.

It was in Vancouver that I picked up a kayak. This was back in my camping phase after leaving Mount Eisenhower and hitch-hiking across BC. I was Nicholas at the time, my first alias, though I still had my old driver's license with me. It might have been my ambiguity, this internal ambiguity of having two current identities, or it might just have been the fact that Nicholas was my first effort, but when the Chinese guy I bought the kayak from dropped me off at the Tsawassen ferry he had the gall to say to me, "Good luck, Nicholas, or whoever you are". That's pretty bad, isn't it, Reader, when you can't even convincingly state your false name?

It had been part of the purchase deal with that guy that he would help me do some running around and then cart me and the kayak to Tsawassen, thus I was pretty well equipped and supplied for my watery sojourn upon leaving Vancouver. The ferry people deal with idiots all the time, so they were all very kind and helpful to me. They didn't make any big deal at all out of me having this ten-foot watercraft with its double bladed paddle onboard along with my other stuff. (Good thing I wasn't trying to get on a plane!) They were so kind-hearted, in fact, that upon docking one of them insisted on packing me and everything into her car, kayak hanging halfway out the trunk, and getting me to an appropriate spot for launching nearby. It was dark by then and she had worried that maybe I'd be better off if she took me to a provincial park or some such place, but she had already been too nice altogether and I couldn't let her do that.

I would highly recommend a kayaking tour along the east shore of Vancouver Island, or anywhere else mildly wildernessy, for anyone wanting to just get away from it all and get in touch with self and nature, and life in general. But you do have to cut yourself off entirely—no cell phone, no stopping at coastal towns to call home, no buying newspapers, no radio to listen to, no et cetera, just you, yourself and you, and the otters frolicking in the water around you, and the raccoons washing their shrimp at the water's edge and casting an eye on you now and then to make sure you aren't about to leap out of the kayak and try to jack them for their lunch, and the bald eagles keeping watch over all from their immensely tall piney perches looming over the water (when they aren't gliding above on wings that grow large—larger than you would ever think a bird's wings could grow—as they soar silently past).

My nautical wanderings weren't particularly focused. For the first few days I drifted south. I had had the vague idea initially of following the entire west coast down to Baja. (Yes, I did say that, Reader. Baja. I was so tired of being cold—you are going to be cold part of every single day you camp out in the Canadian Rockies, high summer or not—that all I thought of at times was just getting myself to some nice, warm desert to proceed with the camping experience). However, after I paddled my kayak (my river kayak, I might add) out to that private island a couple miles offshore from between Sidney and Victoria, the one with the Beware of Dogs and No Trespassing signs, I realized that not only would I not be coasting all the way to Baja (I had already coasted south from the ferry terminal for a day or so at that point), but even the little bit of island-hopping using Saturna and the others to get back to the mainland was entirely beyond sensible in my wave-tossed little coracle. I then had even worse trouble crossing back again from that island the couple miles to where I had started from, what with the wind whipping up a little and the waves coming in a cross-hatch pattern from two different directions. That was a lot like skiing moguls, a black diamond mogul slope about three miles long—and I suck at moguls! First I'd be breaking a monster wave—maybe a three-footer—on my starboard bow, and then before I had time even to raise my hands and express jubilation at my survival a behemoth would slam into me broadside at port. I was flotsam out there. I felt like a cockroach in a urinal fighting the flush. By the time I did eventually make it back to shore I was drained mentally every bit as much as physically. Not having had the mental safety net of counting on, or wanting, society—like here, the Coast Guard—to bail me out, I really felt the full impact out there of self-reliance. On top of that, as a dummy who had gone too far out on the ice to be reached by society's benevolent, rescuing hands in time anyways, and who kept feeling the ice crack and heave under him as he scurried and scampered to the left and to the right, I experienced a very interesting, situational—and situationally absolute—form of existentialism out there made even more poignant by the clear sight on the shore of some houses in a quiet, calm and peaceful little bourgeois community, so close to me yet so very far away, further than far.

I went as far south as Victoria (Oak Bay, I think), and then I retraced my path. I didn't like the currents one bit rounding the point down there. Vicious, very vicious. A lot of work and struggle for very little headway. After my island crossing experience I was quite leery about really open water and I tended to take the long way around as I hugged the coastline. However, by the time I got back up to where I had started, near the ferry terminal, I knew a lot better what I was and wasn't capable of and so I set out, early one morning when the seas were relatively placid, for an island three or four miles to the north and east. I think the island's name was Patricia, or something like that, but I thought of it as my own personal little Treasure Island, a real gem of an island. In many ways that was just the sort of place for a camper like me.

There was a dock at the south end of Treasure Island, but I skipped past it. (People, you know? I wanted seclusion, privacy. Remember, Reader: I'm not yet traveling, I'm still camping, halfway camping.) So instead I paddled east around the island and found myself a nice cove that was exactly what young Hawkins had ordered. No pirates, no sailors, no squires, just the lap of the waves, the cries of the seagulls, the chatter of the squirrels and the rustling of the leaves brought on by the stray breeze now and then. Peace and quiet. A chance for me to stop and figure out what I was doing. Not that I did, really.

It's funny. I had been going hard for quite a while by then, pushing myself at a punishing rate ever since leaving Calgary—ever since leaving Houston a few days before that, really. My days had been long, stressful, and exhausting; and my nights had been short or non-existent. So, what did I do when I found this quiet and restful haven? I sat down on the sand by a piece of driftwood, looked at the trees flanking the shore and got bored. An hour or so of R&R and I was, if not good to go, at least ready to go. Sitting around there twiddling my thumbs didn't feel like it was furthering my interests in any way. I wanted action. Moreover, I had yet to embrace the pre-industrial mindset; so sleeping in the daytime, no matter how much I needed it, wasn't even a conceptual possibility at that point.

Blame it on the boredom, Reader, or maybe it was the mid-day sun weakly beating down on me that addled my brain, but I eventually broke down and cooked a meal. Man, I hate cooking! Do chimpanzees cook? How about dolphins? Or sparrows? Or lions? Of course not! None of them cook. So why do I have to find myself a member of the one, single, solitary species—out of how may? A million or so?—that insists on this abysmal, unnatural waste of time and effort? First you have to prepare the food for cooking—wash it up, measure it out, cut it up and all that—and the very thought of doing so fills me with supreme exasperation. (Have we not teeth? And hands with which to place food between our teeth? We're already miles ahead of birds there. Have you ever watched a bird pecking around on the ground using nothing more than his beak to net his daily calories? And he's making it, isn't he?—When we aren't DDTing him into the ground. And he's probably looking twice as healthy, in his own bird-like way, as the overwhelming majority of us are). Then, after this food preparation, you have to do the actual cooking—which is even twice as bad! They talk about watching paint dry, like that's some sort of baseline comparison for boredom intensity. Well, have you ever watched rice boil? Or just water? Like, yawnsville! You're standing there tapping your foot thinking, "It's not like we're at 10,000 feet elevation here. Hell-ooo-ooo? Can we get a little churn action? Even just a few tiny little bubbles perspiring off the sides of the pot?... Okay, give me just one bubble, for propriety's sake, and I will declare it a boil."

As if food preparation and cooking aren't already bad enough, you've got table setting as well. To someone with a genuine appreciation for the natural world, this is downright agony. Every single dish and utensil you set out on the table is just one more cursed dish or utensil that you are going to have to wash a half hour, maybe an hour, later. It's inevitable, the First Law of Mesodynamics: set it out and you're setting yourself up. A terror lurking at the table and looming ever larger as the meal progresses, so that finally, when all else is done, you reach the climax of your misery: the clean-up—table, dishes, utensils and, worst of all, pots and pans (not to mention containerizing the scraps and placing them in the refrigerator).

Can you see where I'm coming from, Reader? Peel away the layers of culture and it becomes apparent what an enormous waste of time and effort we have here when good nutrition is within reach of our two hands and twenty-eight or so teeth. If you must cook, then at least do it like the Arabs and eat with your hands out of a communal bowl.

So anyway, not having any water left with me to boil the rice in, I peered around my cove for the outlet of a brook or stream. No such luck. (As it turned out, the island was too small for permanent flowing water and the only source there was a centrally located well). That was okay, though, because not only am I innovative, but I am efficient as well. Right there in the cove itself was all the water I could possibly need, and it was already salted, thus saving me one step. Taking the pot from my packsack, I filled it with water and then made a little driftwood fire in the sand to cook over.

Yes, Reader, it took me forever to cook that rice. You think getting water to reach a boil in a microwave is excruciatingly slow. Try it over a campfire, with your stomach growling and nothing else to do but stand around and watch for that first bubble. When I finally saw it—I think—after about two hours, I added a cup of long-grained rice and hunkered down for the long haul. As long as I could keep in mind that this was a project, and not a chore, I would be cool no matter how long it might take. It's not like I had anything else to do for the rest of the day, safe and sound as I was in my private little cove out there on the far side of Treasure Island. I needed the rest time anyway.

The sun was still in the sky when I finally declared my rice ready. It may have been a tad on the crunchy side, but that's just al dente, right? I was famished. A pot of rice might not seem like the height of culinary delight, but I was more than ready for a hot meal. I had been eating fruits, vegetables and prepared foods exclusively for the past couple weeks. I had even experimented with brown sugar—straight. (I had reasoned to myself that they use straight glucose in IVs, so brown sugar was roughly equivalent.)

So what was the moment of discovery like? How complete was my gastronomic ecstasy upon partaking of the fruits of my culinary labors? Oh, Reader! ... Reader, Reader, Reader... you are going to think I am a picky eater after all the effort that went into preparing that erstwhile rice feast.—And it is true that I am a little bit picky when others are doing the cooking; it can't be helped (they need the guidance). But never when it is myself who is doing the cooking (or, more often, the can-opening).— So, no, I can definitely say that I wasn't being picky when, after two or three bites of that sodden mess, I heaved the entire potful into the cove to let the fish see what they could do with it. Drinking seawater all day long, they should have been able to stomach that briney crap. I sure couldn't. I almost vomited—actual vomit—just trying to get those couple bites down. Salt may be a good and necessary thing, and pre-salted water might seem in principle a useful efficiency, but I can tell you it sure didn't work out the way I thought it would. So it was back to brown sugar out of the bag for me. (I think I still had some crackers to go with it at that point).

Treasure Island would have been a fun place for a boys' club camp-out. Finding the water well was like going on a treasure hunt. It took me maybe forty-five minutes. A family had tried to set up a farm there on the island fifty or a hundred years ago, but it didn't end up working out. I'm not sure why, the place seemed so ideal. It was them who had dug or drilled the well, and in that part of the island the trees had been cleared to make room for farmland and orchards. To get to it, all I had to do was walk west until I hit the main north-south trail leading to it, but I had to go cornerwise a little southish because I don't think the trail went the whole distance of the island. After I replenished my water supply (and myself) and got the taste of brine out of my mouth and mind, I took a little tour around the north half of the island, first taking a trail to the shore roughly opposite of my cove and then hugging the shore as much as possible till I arrived back at base. I really liked the place, and the seclusion, and at first I really had planned to kick back and rest up for a few days; but between plain old restlessness—the urge, you know, to get on with the adventure, and even just to get on with things—and getting eaten half to death by mosquitoes through the night, I decided at sun-up to push on towards Nanaimo and the ferry to Horseshoe Bay.

I was getting a lot better at kayaking out on open-water by then. Doing the crossing northward from Treasure Island didn't phase me at all and by mid-morning I was back to coasting, whether on Vancouver Island itself or the big ones close in to it like Saltspring and Thetis. My trip thus to Nanaimo may have been rigorous, but it was relatively pleasant and uneventful—except for Nanaimo Narrows.

Nanaimo Narrows. Simply recalling the name makes me shudder. It was one of the few times in my life when I have felt genuinely and overwhelmingly out of my depth. You would wonder why, Reader, if you could see the setting; it is so idyllic. There is a good-sized island—I can't remember which one—tight in against Vancouver Island there, so close that they could easily join the two with a bridge. By this time I had gained a healthy appreciation for (if not yet a deep understanding of) the tides and the nasty currents they can create. Looking ahead on my map to this tight little bottleneck, I knew it was going to be a beast if I hit it with the tide heading the wrong way. Therefore, I did my best to keep an eye on the tidal situation around me as I approached these narrows. I intended to mount my assault on them when it would be clear sailing. I still don't know if I miscalculated my timing there—like, completely—or if it's just that that is a spot where the flow is perpetually in one direction and varies only in intensity—in which case I would hate to have seen what it could have been like at its nastiest.

Closing in on the narrows I could feel the tug of the current against me increasing dramatically. That surprised me, as I was expecting to be gliding over relatively slack water. I even considered stopping where I was and giving the tide a chance to switch phase, the current was getting so strong, but I figured it might only change for the worse, besides which, the shoreline looked fairly inhabited and thus not overly inviting. As I pushed on it very rapidly became hard work, brutally hard work, just trying to make any headway at all. That simply amazed me.

You've got to remember, Reader, I'm in a kayak. This is a far lighter, more agile, quicker craft than any other muscle powered watercraft out there. Not being a sea-kayak had been a definite disadvantage on open water, but where I was now, a river kayak was optimal. Yet, even in my river kayak these narrows were throwing me around like nothing. In fact, where I was, there in Nanaimo Narrows, was for all means and purposes a short stretch of ferocious river. In the worst section of it I had to hug the shore so tightly—just to get even a slight bit of relief from the stronger current only a little further out—that I was pushing with my left blade off rocks as often as I was paddling with it. Even a lousy two or three feet further out into the channel and I would have been toast. Once I had chosen this course I was pretty much committed with turning back no longer an option; I had no room even to turn around. There was about five feet of brutal current that I had a shot at overcoming, bordered—with virtually no transition—by murderous current daring me to turn my ten-foot of craft broadside just once, even just to give it the nose at the slightest of angles beyond the critical. Just once, just one little slip on my part: that's all it was looking for. I would have been at the mercy of the current, rippling with vicious eddies over rocks encrusted with razor sharp barnacles, for as long as it took me to accelerate enough to regain steering. Best-case scenario in the event of a roll would have seen a wet and bedraggled me successfully extracting myself from that churn and spending the next two hours salvaging what I could find of my possessions from along the shoreline down current.

Those narrows aren't that long, just a few hundred yards at their tightest stretch, but they felt endless to me. I fought and fought, inch by inch. Every time the shoreline jutted out I had to exert every ounce of energy I had just to get around the jut. Such juts got worse and worse the further up I went into that tightening funnel. A blade skittering across a rock without purchase soon became unforgiving, every bit of propulsion was so crucial.

I may have made it through Nanaimo Narrows entirely without portage. It was a struggle, all but beyond me as it was, and I think that the worst was still yet to come. All the same, I may have made it if I had tried. However, I did not try. What stopped me from trying, Reader? Was it simply reason, me recognizing that the risk was rapidly coming to outweigh the gain? How clever and rational that would have been of me!—But, no, it wasn't any such detached contemplation that led me to make the right choice there. It was actually my interaction with another member of my own species (an interaction of which he—this other—was completely incognizant) that broke my dogged concentration and led me to consider scrambling over the rocks along the shore to overcome those last few yards of the passage (and that's all it was, insurmountable though it may have been for me – the fewest of yards reeking of infinity).

Power-boaters! Sep grouches about them all the time. If you ever want to get in the good graces of some sailor, Reader, all you have to do is make a disparaging comment about power-boaters and you'll have made a friend for life. (But be warned: you will also have just let yourself in for a two-hour harangue on the subject). Anyway, like I said, I have listened to Sep curse power-boaters a million times, but I never had any gut understanding of his feeling on the subject until that day in Nanaimo Narrows. There I was, dead beat and summoning up my last reserves for a very iffy assault on the final two and most brutal juts yet before I would at last be out of that neck and into settled water once more, when all of a sudden this supertanker comes steaming out of nowhere behind me at full speed up the narrows casting this massive wake I could have surfed on had I had a surfboard instead of a kayak. It was like being on some kind of a circus ride. One moment I am struggling valiantly against the current alone, the next I am bobbing up and down like a cork and being slammed against the rocks I was just skirting.

I was actually really lucky that I had been in a jog just approaching a jut, rather than out on a jut, when this wake hit me. It threw me around and nearly rolled me as it was. I would have been mincemeat had I been totally exposed right then to the full current. That made me stop and collect my wits. I pulled myself right in against the rocks and jostled against them while the last aftershocks of the power-boat spent themselves out. Having my concentration broken like that may in fact have been a blessing because it gave me the chance and forced me to consider making my final assault on the narrows by land rather than by sea. Getting out of my kayak there was the only real difficulty with that option—and it was a real difficulty, mind you—in contrast to the very serious difficulties of continuing on as I was, along with the unnecessary perils. So I made the obvious decision and thus completed my conquest of Nanaimo Narrows with a whimper instead of a bang. (Yes, I know, Reader, very unHollywood! Remember though, that this is a work of fiction, so it need not have any bearing on your perception of reality). Boy, was I glad to be through! After that, my glide into Nanaimo, even including a tangle with a logjam that would have enjoyed crushing me to death, was child's play.

Chapter 15

You know how I told you what nice memories I have of LA, Reader, even though on closer inspection there really wasn't all that much nice to remember? Part of that is innate optimism, to be sure. But the more important factor is simply my being an island by that time. I can't tell you how wonderful being an island is. I would wish the same for you, and for everyone, if it weren't for the price to be paid in getting here. It is such a feeling of liberation, of individuality. I may have no safety net to catch my fall, but neither do I have anyone directing or restricting my movements in any way. The social contract? That's history. I obey the law now simply out of expedience, not because I have any further moral duty to do so. How can an excommunicant be required to observe mass? Or take communion? Or pay Caesar his tithe? I am a free man, the freest of the free.

Perhaps the greatest thing of all in being an island is how it has opened my eyes as to the fundamental things of life. I drifted through my twenties trying to figure it all out. Life! Meaning! Purpose! Yet I seemed to be getting no further than anyone else—and everyone else was as lost in the dark as I was, that much I could tell. Metaphysics was a major distraction, and understandably so since—if I'm not mistaken—God does in fact exist. Materialism, on the other hand, was just the opposite for me: it was something which I had always dismissed outright yet it has proved instead to be something that cannot be so ignored, something that cannot be left unaccounted for. However, there is only one correct approach to Mammon and verily, verily I say unto you, Reader, it is easier for a camel to thread the eye of a needle than for Western Society to make this approach. Our current deluded embrace of materialism is so complete, so entrenched, that I can't see it taking anything short of a massive catastrophe—or ten—to jolt us out of our stupor, and even then we'd probably let the sirens lull us back into it the first chance we got, or at least we'll look back on this delirium as the halcyon days of Western civilization. Pitiful!

So, what is the meaning of life then, Reader? Is that what you are wanting me to tell you? Is that what I am wanting to tell you, are you wondering? I've just been talking about this great big enlightenment I've had. So what is it? What is life all about?

Sorry, Reader, all that is a secret. Only islands are worthy of such knowledge. You yourself must pay the price and prove yourself worthy to enter this priesthood. We are a holy priesthood, the leavening of mankind. True knowledge and wisdom such as ours is by its very nature veiled, open only to the chosen few.

Ha, ha, ha! I'm kidding, Reader. There's nothing I hate more than all that esoteric mumbo-jumbo. Ignoramuses trying to cloak their ignorance with riddles, seeking to hide it as much from themselves as everyone else. Certainly I'll tell you what I can, but I can't give you a full answer, or even a satisfyingly complete one, because I can't honestly say that it is all that clear yet in my mind. I mean, it isn't. However, whereas in the past I was working with a flawed paradigm, I now know what the flaws are in that paradigm so that it is only a matter of time and contemplation for me to develop a whole new paradigm and come to understand it fully. Rather I should say, this new paradigm is already in my mind and now it's just a matter of discovering and exploring it fully. And furthermore, I should not even describe it as new because I am positively convinced that it was always there, that it is there in my own mind and in most everyone's mind, and that it is only the accumulated debris of millennia upon millennia of mankind's explosive technological development, along with the accompanying social upheaval every step of the way, that has buried the truth and concealed it from us.

Can you see then, Reader, the advantages an island has in rediscovering this foundation of our being? I was cut off from society. I have lived the life of a true savage, urban though I have remained most of the time. I trod the paths of Adam, that Adam when Eve was not yet so much as a tickling in his side. I was, for a time, the only man left on earth. Omega Man. Alone. Everything mine, to have, to hold, to comprehend without further delusion. Nobody knows the animal—the nature—within us, within every one of us, like I, the island, do: not the mightiest leader of mankind, with his finger perpetually on the button that could eradicate human society from the face of the earth; nor the basest transgressor of the laws of mankind, whether locked away in his dungeon or roaming free to terrorize his fellow man. I alone, the island, have known complete solitude, have felt what it is to be the entire manifestation of the human race, have understood the responsibility of carrying the whole species in my own bosom, on my own two shoulders, shoulders so frail, so magnificently strong. This is what it is to be an island. And regarding the search for truth: no lies from others because there are no others; and similarly no lies to others; no lies even to self because self is now all-encompassing, thus all-purifying; nothing but the need for reality, pertinent reality, simple and unvarnished—otherwise known as truth.

Hollywood as truth: how laughable! But, really, how laughable is it? Is the Frenchman slitting his wrists any less senseless than the American wallowing in his beer? Unless you have a viable alternative, the object of your criticism is also your point of reference. We can laugh at, sneer at and despise Hollywood—Tinseltown!—all day long, yet at the end of the day where are we?—what do we have to put in place of its romanto-materialism? If the answer is, "Nothing," even dressed up into, "Nihilism," then of course our laughter cannot help but ring hollow. Whether or not I am correct in ascribing this outlook, this dilemma, to society in general, it is an accurate description of my own personal outlook prior to my becoming an island. So let me share with you, Reader, the two important things I have learned on this score.

Matter is real. Thus far, at least, Hollywood is right.—What I am saying is that it is wrong—I had been wrong—to discount the material world and look solely to the metaphysical realm for meaning.—Where Hollywood, Anglo-American humanism, goes wrong is in making human sensation the yardstick of good and bad. With such a standard, orgasm becomes the ultimate good and pain the gauge of bad. Even death now is only bad insofar as it causes pain, whether to the dying themselves or to their loved ones in bereavement. (You think I exaggerate here, Reader? Look at the way the US Supreme Court disallows those forms of capital punishment that cause pain to the recipient but okays the pain-free variety. I remain a little mystified about the irony of a black fly in Chardonnay—or rain on your wedding day—but if this isn't ironic, I don't know what is! Like, "Please hold still, Mr. Evildoer, while the executioner—errr, the execution-giver, I mean to say—administers the prescribed dosage of new and improved strychnine; you should not experience any pain or discomfort, but if you do then please alert us immediately, within say the next forty-five seconds, and we will be more than happy to abort this particular procedure and recommence your termination with some more acceptable method.")

The problem with making human sensation the standard of good and bad is that technological development over the past few centuries has steadily undermined its validity. Look at sugar, for example: Tastes very good. Makes desserts delectable. Enhances the flavor of even main course items like bread. So, according to the human sensation standard, it should be strictly a good thing, right? Yet obesity is not good, correct? Nor is tooth decay, correct? And both of these things are direct results of consuming sugar, and regulating such consumption with the barometer of human sensation. So what's going on here? Technology is enabling us to short-circuit the hardware that we are equipped with, thus circumventing its design. Sugar and other sources of calories, a much-needed commodity for all mammals, have historically been scarce enough that our sensors for them are finely tuned and our brains are wired to respond very positively to such sensations. That's useful when you can barely get enough calories even actively pursuing all available opportunities, and not merely useful but downright critical in a borderline (equilibrium) existence where a lackadaisical attitude could result in death. However, in our altered reality where we are inundated with food calories it no longer makes sense to regulate our intake of them by the sensory apparatus we have that was designed for an existence in pristine nature. Yet that, by making human sensation the standard of good and bad, is exactly what we are doing, whether on the scale of the average, unthinking individual or that of the highly analytical and calculating corporate entities of Madison Avenue.

Orgasm is another excellent study. Fleeting though it may be, it is the ultimate positive sensation. As such it has been raised on a pedestal by Hollywood and whole swathes of our society. Lacking any purpose in life they find more compelling than this, they have fixed on it and orient themselves and their lives according to its dictates. Sex is no longer a biological function resulting in self-replication (the one certain form of immortality, even if diluted, de-individualized and uncertain in the long term). Instead it is the vehicle for attaining orgasm. Therefore, anything goes, just as long as the result is orgasm: whips, chains, oral, anal, twosomes, threesomes, twelvesomes, homo, hetero, lesbo, man on sheep, donkey on woman, soft porn, hard porn, kiddie porn—even drugs like cocaine and ecstasy will do, despite the synthetic nature of the orgasms they produce. (The only thing Hollywood hasn't got the guts to do yet is openly put children on the altar. But they will, Reader, mark my words, they will. Step One towards this end will be the portrayal of child pornographers as misguided yet sincere. Step Two will be the introduction into mainstream discourse of the concept of "intergenerational love". And Step Three will be the publicizing of children speaking out for their "right" to "love" whomever they wish. From that point it's a slam-dunk. Society will have sacrificed its last value without even realizing that the negotiation and argument were underway. But I digress.)

The problem with orienting ourselves around orgasm, with making it the compass of our society, is that orgasm is not a purpose in and of itself. It is only a sensor, an inducement leading us to pursue the actual purpose involved, that being self-replication. For us to neglect this real purpose in our obsession with the sensation that is designed to result in it is another way in which we are short-circuiting ourselves. Instead of being sensor-informed, living sensor-informed, we allow ourselves to become sensor-driven—and that, dear Reader, is really, truly pitiful.

The obsession with orgasm is essentially materialistic, but it is related to the other fundamental fallacy promulgated by Hollywood. Romanticism. You cannot watch a movie out of Hollywood without being exposed to romance. This is a key element of the alchemist's cinematic formula. What is interesting about this—about both romanticism and its presence in said formula—is that romanticism is at heart metaphysical. Therefore, despite the bridge between it and materialism that orgasm provides, there is still a basic and ineradicable antagonism between these two belief systems cohabiting within the house of Hollywood: the materialistic wedded to the metaphysical.

Metaphysical? Romanticism is metaphysical? Did I really mean to say that? Yes, Reader, I did. As commonplace and everyday as romanticism may seem, and be, it is nevertheless entirely metaphysical in nature. Love at first sight. The quest for Mr. Right. She knew, she just knew, that he was, he had to be, The One. Two souls joined in a mystical union for all time. The bliss eternal that we all know to be complete blarney yet which we vicariously imbibe with every product of Hollywood we consume.

Romanticism is the offspring, perhaps the bastard offspring, of

Judaeo-Christian thought. You see the seeds of it in the Old Testament even from the very beginning with Adam and Eve and then gaining steam in the Song of Solomon. Jesus contributed significantly to its development in emphasizing the joining together of a man and a woman to become one flesh (and arguing thus the theologically illegitimate nature of divorce). But it is only in the Middle Ages, with the troubadours and their crypto-Gnostic rebuttal of Christianity proper, that we see the advent of a distinct form, even if early, of full blown romanticism. No longer do you see merely the courtship rituals of the procreative relationship dressed up in the finery of passion, or the procreative relationship itself imbued with the legitimacy of divine sanction, but instead you see the subtle morphing or devolution of this definitively procreative relationship into a relationship where procreation is peripheral and entirely optional. No longer do we have a natural relationship where a man and woman come together with the common interest of producing by their joint efforts some biological immortality for themselves, a very potent interest; instead we have a fundamentally metaphysical relationship where the relationship itself, the union of soul now, rather than flesh, and the purported self-transcendence inherent in such union, is all that ultimately matters. Procreation remains a powerful, visceral argument, and romanticism doesn't hesitate to exploit it, so that more often than not the narratives that Hollywood provides us result in the coupling of virile men with fertile women, but when was the last time you saw a movie, Reader, culminating in childbirth? The production of offspring in romanticism is entirely beside the point. Happily ever after is achieved, fully and with the permanence of eternity, in the union of two souls. Anything subsequent to that, including procreation, is post-narrative and completely immaterial.

I sound a little down on romanticism, don't I, Reader? Well, I am a little down on romanticism. I have explored it fully and found it wanting. Mene, mene, tekel upharsim. In fact, I have found it more than wanting. The saving grace of most metaphysical belief systems is that they further life, the life and interests of their belief community, at least. This is not so with romanticism, which in its purest form is the very abnegation of life. No greater love hath a man than that he lay down his life for his friend. That is the fundamental tenet of romanticism—that, as opposed to Christianity's (and Judaism's) Do unto others as you would have them do unto you. Imagine Christianity without the Church, without the fellowship of believers, with nothing but the cross: anchorites perched alone atop their poles. The object of romanticism is something akin to that: the exclusion and suppression of everything in life except for the object of one's love, so that this object, this person, becomes everything—and this process is made exponentially more fascinating and meaningful by the reciprocal action of one's love vis-à-vis oneself. Yet, fascinating and meaningful as the process may be (we are talking here about the exploration, the mutual exploration, of the human mind, an incredibly complex and powerful working), the result is decidedly less than the promised self-transcendence, the anticipated encompassing of the infinite, the expected grasping of the ineffable. When all is said and done, one knows one's love with exquisite intimacy, and one knows oneself intimately better than before, but one has not approached God, one has not seen His face, or even the back of His head—and this also one knows, knows perhaps most of all, certainly most poignantly of all. So discover the truth of the matter for yourself if you must, Reader, and it may very well be that you must, but in the end you will see that I am right in what I have just said, and just how precisely right I am. So much for romanticism.

Can you see, then, that the alternative to Hollywood's romanto-materialism is centered on biology? Dependent as it has come to be on human sensation for authority, Anglo-American humanism quite understandably finds itself leery of biology—raw, undomesticated biology in the rough with its nettles and teeth, and its toxins and stings and claws and howling. This antagonism toward genuine biology, the full press of life, began to gain steam a couple hundred years ago, which was about the same time when we were doing our best to purge ourselves of all metaphysical argumentation and attachments. These two processes, the divorce of humanity from the rest of biology and the eradication of religious thought, created the context in which romanticism was then able to explode onto the scene the way it did—romanticism, with its metaphysical nature hidden behind a guise of—irony of ironies!—faux naturalism!

So in identifying our orientation around human sensation as the fundamental problem, I am effectively removing not only human sensation, but both it and romanticism, as impediments to our further progress. I have thus entered a whole new paradigm. The way is now made clear to elevate biology to a position of primacy, and this in both the material realm we occupy without question and the metaphysical which may not even exist. It is this enlightenment that has been for me the greatest blessing of having been an island, of having known absolute liberty—liberty of being and liberty of thought—as only an island can know it, absolute liberty and absolute responsibility.

Chapter 16

The sun is coming up now, Reader. Soon I'll be in La Paz. But I know I mentioned a particularly exciting episode I had in the fall. There should be just enough time for me to share that with you before I have to close. It all started in an anonymous little city on the prairie. It all started there for me, that is to say. The entire production had been running for quite some time at that point, but despite the fact that I had the lead role around which everything else revolved I was oblivious to it all, dummy that I was. And it was only sheer good luck and the happiest of odd chances that led to my suddenly gaining awareness of the danger I was in, the spider's web that was being woven around me.

"You want another sandwich?" Four simple words, as unassuming as any other four words out there: You want another sandwich? But if it weren't for those four words and the conversation they initiated I guarantee you, Reader, I wouldn't be sunning myself here this fine Pacific morning on a ferry in México approaching the tip of the Baja peninsula.

I was sitting in a Greydog terminal looking at the baloney sandwich and container of juice I had just been given as a courtesy for there being some delay in my departure. This trip was not going overly well. First there had been a blizzard in Wyoming, leading to slowdowns and an unscheduled stop there, and now I was being treated to an unexpected stopover here. The baloney didn't help matters. I drank the orange juice and decided to toss the sandwich; but then I saw a black guy at the next table over that I recognized from the bus I'd been on, and he was wolfing down his sandwich as if it was his first meal in a week. I was so tired and worn out that I really didn't feel like chatting with anyone, and he probably felt the same, but after I gave him my sandwich it was one of those awkward situations where you can hardly help but exchange a few words.

This guy was traveling home to St. Louis from some place where he had been living on the west coast. He was very aware of his surroundings in a way that a fugitive like myself should be. He explained this awareness in the course of the conversation as being the result of having had run-ins with the law on a number of occasions throughout his life. He was 35 or 40 years old. But it was almost the very first thing he said that caught my attention most of all, and "caught my attention" is putting it mildly.

“I wonder who they were after.” Just out of the blue like that as he was munching down the baloney.

“Who?” I asked. Like, what was he talking about?

“You didn’t notice them? The bounty hunters?”

Bounty hunters??!! Every cell in my body went from zero to DefCon 5 in about three nanoseconds. Who were they after? I wonder! What, hadn’t I noticed them? Expletive, no! Expletive, expletive, expletive, expletive! Expletive! I was almost heaving my orange juice and I could hardly even form a word my stomach was suddenly so knotted up, but it wasn’t as if I could let buddy in on my distress. Yet I had to continue this conversation not only to keep up appearances, but also because I desperately needed whatever information the guy could give me.

Uuuuuuuuhhh, “Huh?” I hoped my face was registering quizzical rather than the frantic I was feeling. I was doing good to get even that one syllable out of my mouth without a chaser of puke following it up.

"Man, I don't know how you could help but have seen them. There were enough of them. I saw four at least. There was the lady with the gray wig, the guy who was sitting just over there till he left to get on an eastbound bus a few minutes ago, and a couple other guys. I guess it's different for people who have never been in trouble with the law." And he proceeded to explain a little, just a little, about his past.

Breathe, Gary, breathe! And I did untense a fair bit as buddy chattered on. His speculations as to the target of the bounty hunter team centered on two different guys who had continued on east. He had had his eye on both of them since Wyoming when we had had the stopover there. (Greydog had first put us all up at a motel and then before night closed in we had gotten back on the bus). To buddy all of this had been a game, a spectator sport of cat and mouse, him being the cat and the bounty hunters being the mice. The only prize he was after was the secret of who they were pursuing. He had even approached one of them at the motel in Wyoming in a wink-wink, nudge-nudge kind of way to try to satisfy his curiosity, but he said that he had been given the brush-off. (Good thing!)

When buddy ran out of steam I asked him a little about the two guys, either of whom he figured was the potential target, and I vaguely recalled fellow passengers fitting the descriptions he gave me. However, when I continued on seeking descriptions of the two bounty hunters he hadn't already described he all of a sudden turned reticent on me and said, "I really shouldn't have said anything about all this."

All right, then. I could see that my pressing him for further info had made buddy a little suspicious of me. No sense in killing the goose that laid the golden egg. Changing the subject I let the conversation proceed a little longer then wind down. I urgently needed a bit of time to myself anyway for some serious analysis and planning.

Number One: Was I the target? Or was this just coincidence, some other fugitive making a cameo here and causing some seriously unnecessary confusion and turmoil for me? After all, from what buddy said the team had continued on east and so the storm was past, wasn't it?... But could I seriously believe this was only a coincidence? Like, how often do bands of legalized thugs run around the country stalking people on the Greydog? This, precisely, was not something I had expected to encounter as a fugitive, yet it certainly was within the realm of possible. So I concluded that although it would be really great if it truly was just a coincidence, I would be a complete fool to treat it as such and merely continue on my merry way.

So Number Two: What was I to do? Toadsuck USA is actually a fair-sized burg, but it felt small to me. I felt really exposed in such a small-feeling place like I had nowhere to hide there. Of course running, escaping any trap that may have been closing around me, was the obvious thing to do. How I wished I was in LA, sprawling LA with its crush of humanity, or Vancouver, or Miami, where I had been headed! In places like those every bus, every cab, every mall is an asset to the fugitive, and the downtown core most of all. But there in Toadsuck with its empty shops and deserted streets I might as well have been a solitary traveler on a treeless plain wearing neon, I was so lacking in cover.

Whatever I did, I had to play it cool. If I had been under surveillance then I was still under surveillance. No two ways about that. I went outside the station for a few minutes to get some fresh air, and I even took a stroll up the street for a block or two to see if there was anything about the place that might suggest some options for me. But I was careful to act casual, very casual, the whole time. I didn't want to set off any alarm bells and force my adversaries' hand.

If these people had been watching me since at least Wyoming then surely they knew that my bus ticket was to a city two stops from where we were. (It wasn't all the way to Miami, in case you wondered, Reader. That would have been indiscreet.) So if they had been content with merely stalking me thus far, rather than pouncing on me, they likely felt no urgency about grabbing me prior to my reaching that supposed destination. Good! So hopefully I had a little breathing space.—Yet I couldn't count on too much: I was good for one more stop, but that last one could very well have a welcoming party ready and waiting for me. Theoretically I had to choose then between Toadsuck, where I was, and Possumtrot, where I would reach next, as the staging area for giving these creeps the slip. The choice was obvious, though. Possumtrot was no LA, but it was definitely a scale or two up from Toadsuck.

I spent the rest of the morning chilling in the Greydog station and early in the afternoon I hopped on the bus to Possumtrot. As I was waiting in line to get on I saw the guy who had earlier disappeared, apparently—but obviously not after all—leaving on an eastbound bus, the one who had been described to me by the black guy as one of the bounty hunters. I really wasn't thrilled to see him, as you can well imagine, Reader, having still held out hope that there might be something to the coincidence theory, but I couldn't honestly feel the least surprised, either. Noticing the black guy, who was also taking that bus, as I passed the seat he was settling into, I tried to say Hi, but he only glared at me and turned away without a word. I took that in itself as another confirmation of my fears—as if I needed any more!

The bus ride to Possumtrot was uneventful. I spent the time planning and preparing, but you wouldn't have thought it to see me. That I was under some kind of surveillance was a given, so it was critical that I do nothing to raise suspicion. My main decision was what to keep with me upon hightailing it. That meant reviewing my trip so far to analyze the possibility of having been tagged with some form of electronic surveillance—a bug or a beacon. The prognosis wasn't great. The stop in Wyoming had been bad, in this regard. All the passengers had been checked into the motel late in the morning. Having had a room to myself, there would have been no worries (after-the-fact worries) had I just stayed in my room and rested. But I didn't. After showering and shaving I had left the motel and wandered across the highway to a mall where I had gotten a haircut. My knapsack and all my stuff had been sitting in my room the whole time, every bit of it an inviting target for miniaturized electronics. (I don't exactly know how small such devices can get, but I do know they can get down to the size of a matchstick or a dime). This meant that every bit of it was tainted. I didn't have the luxury there on the bus to inspect everything—or even anything—because that would have been way too obvious. I had even taken off my money belt in the motel and left it hidden there when I went out. Stupid, stupid, stupid! That meant I'd have to go to the washroom at the back of the bus and visually inspect all my money. Losing my belongings was no big deal—they were all disposable enough, replaceable enough. But the money was another thing altogether. I already told you what tough living LA had been on nothing a day. I preferred not to go through all that again. Besides which, I needed cash just for the upcoming flight—and I'm not talking about a plane ride. I had no set plan to follow upon reaching Possumtrot, but most of the possibilities, the better ones, involved a fair bit of hemorrhage to the old pocketbook. So I could let everything else go, even the shirt off my back, but not the money.

I couldn't actually let the shirt go either, as a matter of fact, because making a spectacle of myself in the process of bolting would have been counterproductive. However, as I analyzed things further, I came to realize that even the clothes I was wearing were suspect. After leaving the motel in Wyoming—we had only been there a few hours when they bundled us back onto the bus—a big white guy had sat next to me on the bus. I was disinclined to think he was one of the bounty hunters—surely the black guy would have mentioned one of them having sat by me in the part of our conversation when he was being candid—but I couldn't rule out the possibility, and he did seem like someone who would have fit the profile. Anyway, the bad thing in this regard was that I had dozed a little through the night there on the plains of Nebraska. I really don't sleep while traveling, nor do I sleep sitting up; nevertheless, I couldn't guarantee to myself that I had not slept at all on that bus ride. As improbable as it was that I—any article of my clothing—had been tagged there on that bus, the possibility was there, and was reasonable enough, that I had to incorporate it into my planning. Man, oh man!

My conclusion after this analysis was that I could keep my wallet, my ID and my money. I had to plan on jettisoning everything else, including my beloved money belt and even my shoes (and excellent, comfortable, presentable shoes they were too, basically urban hiking boots). That may sound like overkill, disposing of quite so much, but I was simply working with the odds: some things may have had only a ten percent chance of contamination, some only a one percent chance, yet even that was too high. Why would I want to risk so much as a one percent chance of taking away with me the means of my own apprehension when I could reduce the risk essentially to nil? This situation was, for me, like that of the man on the Titanic who had had to choose between stuffing his pockets with valuable jewels or something more practical and having a greater immediate value. Find yourself in such a situation, Reader, and you'll see that it's a no-brainer—if you've got half a brain.

We got to Possumtrot. No welcoming party, thankfully. It would be a few hours wait until my ostensible connection, so I planned to sit around for a little while and then slip out for some fresh air, never to return. I was glad I had established this pattern of movement in Wyoming and Toadsuck. The station at Possumtrot, however, was just about to close for the night when we reached there—this was a new one for me, a Greydog station in a large city closing for the night?—and so I had to make a quick adjustment to my plans. Unexpected this was, but fortuitous all the same because it made my departure from the station that much less of an occurrence. The bounty hunter who never had actually gotten on the eastbound bus at Toadsuck was near me when the station closing announcement was made and so I made a point of running up to the ticket desk and confirming that my connection would still be leaving at midnight and that I would have no problem getting back into the station and getting on that bus. It wasn't like they were offering me the option of remaining on the premises but I was just playing to the surveillance gallery anyway, easing any concerns they might have had as to my intentions. The last thing I wanted was for their point man to panic and call in the cavalry.

Leaving the station, I walked a few blocks till I found myself at a department store downtown. I had a critical need for this store, to get the shoes, socks, pants, and a shirt that it could supply me. The store itself was about to close but I got what I needed in time. After making my purchases I left there and sauntered casually around the downtown for a few more blocks. I wasn't trying to see if I was being followed. I don't know enough about how shadowing works to be confident one way or another about detecting it. (I guess you already know that, Reader). Moreover, I was pretty certain that I was carrying some kind of beacon; there had been too much opportunity altogether for them to have planted something somewhere in my belongings, besides which, I doubted that they would have permitted me as much freedom of movement as I had already had if they hadn't had some such cause for feeling secure as to my precise whereabouts at all times. In wandering like that, I was really only insuring that the only direct visual observation that there would have been was coming from behind. That way I could turn a corner and have a moment or two free from surveillance. This was all I needed, a few times over, to get out of my clothes and into my new ones. It was twilight by this time and, except for the runners, I had roughly matched the colors of my replacement clothes to what I was wearing, so an observer would have been hard-pressed to take notice of this switcheroo without actually watching me in the act.

At last I was ready for the decisive moment, my big break-out from the surveillance. I had a walletful of money in my pocket. I was wearing an all-new wardrobe. And I was carrying the department store bag full of my contaminated clothes in my right hand and my thoroughly contaminated knapsack over my left shoulder. If I was going to be grabbed—that is to say, if they were good enough, omnipotent, omniscient and omnipresent enough, that they weren't going to be letting me out of their grasp—then it would be happening in the next few minutes.

Was I really under surveillance, Reader? This is a very interesting question. There are some questions in life that cannot be answered definitely in the negative, yet the very act of discovering definite answers to them in the affirmative renders (or would render) them moot. I think of this class of question as the "metaphysical binary" since metaphysical questions naturally fall into it. Not that there was anything metaphysical about the surveillance I was under.

No, Reader, to this day I do not know for sure that I was under surveillance there on that bus trip taking me to Possumtrot. The only definite answer to that question would have been produced by my apprehension. (This is assuming that we can give that team enough credit that they weren't about to do something so stupid as to give themselves away to me directly). The preponderance of the evidence I had supported this surveillance theory, and strongly enough that it demanded I act accordingly. The black guy's report was powerful evidence. The continued presence of the eastbound bus guy was significant. I never saw the lady with the gray wig again, but her even being mentioned in the first place had rung a bell, because I had been struck when I had seen her first get on the bus by how young her face was and so how discordant her long gray hair was (not that I subsequently became suspicious of her for that). I couldn't satisfactorily identify in hindsight the other two alleged bounty hunters from among the busload of people accompanying me (the majority having traveled on that bus from Salt Lake), but I could rule out a bunch of people and I did end up with one strong candidate—and he had gotten on the same bus as me somewhere in Oregon or Idaho (before the Salt Lake connection, that is to say).

Of course, it was also possible that the black guy had just made up the whole thing for fun or that he was merely delusional and had imagined it all. However, for various reasons these possibilities were both extremely unlikely. Left thus with either myself the target of this bounty hunter team or someone else as their target, the most logical conclusion, considering the situation I am in, is that it was me they were after. And that, Reader, is as definite an affirmative as you are ever going to get from any such binary.

So why was I being surveilled rather than simply apprehended? There are a couple possibilities. The first is that whoever was paying the bounty hunters wanted information that they felt they might somehow be able to get from me. I won't bore you with any long tangents here, Reader. Suffice it to say that presumably my apprehension would have been counterproductive toward that end. The other possibility—and very real, ludicrous though it may sound—is that the bounty hunters simply wanted a better jurisdiction, from their point of view, to arrest me in. The States is not like Canada; it is a hodge-podge of fifty different criminal codes, meaning fifty different sets of law codes only vaguely reconciled by the federal Supreme Court and fifty different state-to-state extradition policies. Assuming that the bounty hunters knew the destination of my ticket, it could very well have been that they were just being opportunistic and allowing me enough freedom to get myself into a jurisdiction close to Texas—close whether as to geography or philosophy. So, that I was under surveillance rather than arrest did not surprise me. I was just glad it was bounty hunters who had found me and not the cops because they, the cops, definitely would have just snatched me up without further ado.

The more interesting question for me here is how the bounty hunters had been able to locate me. North America is a big place. Barring appearances on nationally broadcast shows like that cursed 'Unresolved Mysteries', you can remain incognito for pretty much as long as you want (and even such national exposure is manageable if you stay on top of it). All you have to do is be discreet.—And I was discreet, I had been discreet... Though there was an indiscreet phone call I'd made when I was working the apple harvest in the Okanagan. Did I really end up paying for that indiscretion after all with this close call on the road to Possumtrot? I mean, I'll never know, but it is one of two likely explanations. The other possible explanation is that my appearance in the Seattle Greydog station had been noted by some sharp-eyed ticket agent who earned a small cash bonus on the side for alerting whoever. At first glance that might seem rather unlikely, but when you stop and think about it you can see that there are certain chokepoints that someone in my shoes and with my limited means is liable to pass through, Greydog stations in general being one (travel by air, with its greater likelihood of identity scrutinization, really is not to be preferred). From there, if you can narrow down the geographic scope of such chokepoints, you increase your odds many times over of locating the fugitive you want. In my case Seattle was a very logical place to set a trap (or at least a tripwire) because it is the only large city out west close to the border. If the guy who got on the bus in Oregon or Idaho really was a bounty hunter, and if he was the first of that crew to get right on my tail, then that would place him in a reasonably likely time-frame for being the first responder to an alert coming out of Seattle. But, like with my indiscreet phone call from the Okanagan, I am just speculating here and I'm sure I'll never learn the truth of the matter.

Let's get back to Possumtrot now, Reader, and the shadows breathing down my neck there. Since I'm telling you all this you already know that they didn't get me, so I'm not going to try to build up all kinds of suspense on that score. Not that there wasn't any suspense in that regard for me at the time. It's not like I knew it was all going to turn out alright. There I was in a strange city with nothing but the clothes on my back and fifteen hundred bucks or so in my pocket. So far all had gone well in my effort toward extricating myself from the trap that had been closing in on me, but it sure wasn't a done deal yet at that point. I still had to ditch the contaminated stuff I was carrying and put enough distance between me and it before my pursuers came to realize that I was onto them. The most critical issue was visual surveillance, its lack or laxness. I desperately hoped that the primary surveillance was the electronic (the assumed electronic) and that the visual was only secondary. This wasn't just hope out of desperation though, because if surveillance rather than apprehension is one's objective, then it only makes sense to be cautious (in shadowing) and not get so close as to risk exposing oneself to one's target. My path around downtown had been erratic enough that any sensible tail would have pulled back considerably.

The initial break was only one of two critical things, however, that I had to consider right then. The other was maintaining my freedom in the hours following that and then exiting Possumtrot. Why should this latter have been a worry to me? Because as soon as they learned that I had burned them, and I figured that fifteen minutes or so of a stationary beacon would be the longest they would tolerate before sending my tail in to sniff up close, the chances were good as not that my pursuers would call in the cops and make Possumtrot a very hot place indeed for me. The bus station was already out of the question (obviously), likewise the train station and the airport—all those thanks solely to the bounty hunters and their resources. But with the cops in the mix too, suddenly a taxi-ride, and particularly an inter-city taxi-ride (otherwise my first choice), was also out of the question. Nor was I keen to book into a hotel, or even to stand out on the highway trying to thumb a ride out of town. So, as good a start that I was off to, it was still only a start and there would yet be some very serious obstacles for me to overcome.

Alright then, Reader, so I was downtown ready to make my break. I walked around a little longer until I found a nicely situated dumpster. Heaving everything in there, including my coat, I scrammed at a dignified pace and, a couple blocks away, jumped on the first city bus I could find going anywhere. That stretch from the dumpster to the bus was nerve-wracking, being the decisive extended moment revealing to me whether or not I had miscalculated the tightness of any visual surveillance I was under. Luckily, it turned out okay. Either I had calculated correctly, or I was giving them far too much credit anyway (a possibility that I am always aware of yet I never have the luxury to countenance)—or of course the whole thing could all have just been an illusion.

Just having made it onto the bus didn't mean that I was entirely in the clear. Had I been observed boarding the bus it would have been possible for them to resume their surveillance of me, though it would have involved a quick switch from travel by foot to travel by vehicle. So after I had put the downtown core behind me I got off that bus and onto a different one. Only then did I begin to breathe easy. My pursuers would have had to have been superhuman to overcome that final dodge.

With surveillance and pursuit no longer direct threats to me I was able to set aside the evasive tactics and focus instead on extricating myself from the greater Possumtrot area. Being an island, the idea of simply walking out of town didn't phase me at all, even it if looked to take a few days to be out of the danger zone. However, it occurred to me that a bicycle would speed me along at double the pace or more and would offer the added benefit of putting me into a higher tax bracket (for the sake of those who might take note of me as I traveled by). Accordingly, when I reached the Whalemart on the edge of town at the end of the line (yet another bus) I picked out a mountain bike along with all the camping and other supplies I was purchasing there. I was then all set for another nice little commune with nature, me, myself and I and the great outdoors. I had shaken my pursuers and with just a little physical exertion—well, maybe a lot—soon I'd be far enough away that they wouldn't have a chance of picking up my scent again.

Chapter 17

Reader, I hope you do not want me to tell you about my bike-trip across Missouri. I promise it wouldn't make a particularly gripping narrative. I had a run-in with Mother Nature at one point and I was rescued by, of all people, a cop. Some fugitive, eh? Luckily, he didn't take the opportunity to run a check on me. (And why would he bother to on a clean-cut student who was taking a semester off school to see a bit of the country bicycling and camping?) On this excursion I stuck mostly to the winding, two-lane highways that hit every little hole-in-the-wall, but for one good stretch I followed an old railway line that had been transformed into a bike path. That latter was ideal, a real idyll—you get a beautifully graded course to follow, no vehicles trying to run you down, and all the peace and quiet you could want for enjoying the scenery. But, like I said, there really isn't much to tell here, and so I'm not even going to start. I will say, though, that Missourians, rural Missourians, are some of the best people you will find in the whole world. I really mean that.

Anyway, I'm headed to La Paz now because my island days are coming to an end. Come to think of it, in a sense they are over already, for the moment I decided that I was at last ready to turn myself in I laid down the causeway that I will soon be crossing back to the mainland. (Of course if I can convince Sep to help me out with my technology enterprise then I will be putting off anything quite so precipitate as that for a little while yet). So I guess you can say that I'm in another transitional phase opposite to the one I'd been in when I was camping.

After all that I've told you about being an island, the freedom of being an island, the purity of being an island, the illumination of living life as an island, you must be wondering, Reader, why I am willing to give it up now, to surrender this freedom and purity, and to forgo any further illumination that might await me here. Sometimes I wonder myself. Part of it is that I have now fully been an island; I have thus drunk this cup to the dregs and learned the lessons to be learned from this lesson-book. Far more important, though, is the fact that, in being humanity, in being the full incarnation of humanity, I have come at last to appreciate humanity, my fellow man. I have come to realize that, despite being the full incarnation of humanity, I am not the fullest incarnation of humanity. The fullest incarnation of humanity is, in fact, the entirety of humanity, a grand undertaking in which I must take my place and fulfill my role. Yes, I could play this role as Barry, or Ken, or Nicholas, or Kerry, or Cary, or whoever of the forty-odd men I have been over the past year; but as none of them could I perform my part as I will be able to as Gary, the man I have been all my life whatever other verbal identifiers I may have masked myself with over the past few months.

I used to think of myself as a dilettante, and I was a dilettante, proudly so. But I'm not one anymore, I can see that clearly. The occupation of the true dilettante is guerrilla satire. He lives his criticism of society. But when the dilettante's thinking evolves such that out of his criticism of society he develops an alternative program for society, the way of the guerrilla satirist is no longer tenable for him and he must adapt to conventional modes of ideological struggle. The man of inaction—not passively, but actively of inaction—is thus transformed into the man of action, the very man of action. This is what is happening to me. Not only am I no longer a dilettante, but the fact is that I am now quite the opposite. Ennui is a thing of the past for me.

So there you have, Reader, the account of my sojourn as an island. It is coming to an end now as surely as this ferry is pulling up to the dock. Soon I will be tracking Sep down—and this time no pussyfooting around. Then, sometime after that, I will be hopping on a bus to Tijuana, for which I think I may reprise my Hernando Cortez identity (though, come to think of it… that might just have been a contributing factor in my Samuel

Martin ordeal last time around... so maybe it would be best to rethink that bright idea), and then another bus, and another one, and so on until I reach Calgary and the loving arms of Lucifer Lewretch. I will certainly see some lovely scenery along the way. I will even more certainly see some lovely girls, some frustratingly lovely girls with whom I will have these frustratingly pointless proto-romances that I know I won't be following up on. Not for the time being, anyway. Oh, the agony of being an island, Reader! And I've hardly even scratched the surface with the little I've told you on that score. Yesenia, Zoraya, Donna, Marcie, Maricela, Maria Elena, Amber, Marita, Courtney, Judith, Clarissa, Leanna, Victoria, Rosa...

Works by Gary Wilson

Island (the one that wasn't supposed to be)

Gary's first novel, this story follows a young man overtaken by events who finds himself a fugitive fleeing from the law. Although a tale of action, it is in the interludes of thought that we see that this narrative serves as an analysis and criticism of existentialism.

Where Then O Bliss

A prequel to *Island (the one that wasn't supposed to be)*, this romance about the love between an idealistic student and a victim of severe spousal abuse serves as an analysis and criticism of romanticism. See sample chapter below.

Bioism: The Deity of Life

A compilation of essays elucidating the philosophy that Gary has developed, bioism. See sample essay, *The Age of Sophistry*, below.

Relativity Riddled: Inframotionality

A physics model that is an alternative to the standard physics model and overcomes the structural defects of relativity.

Please visit www.garywilson.ca to see more details and the most current listing of the works by Gary Wilson.

About the Author

Gary Wilson is a Canadian, born and raised in Calgary. Moving to Houston in 1996 to study law, he ended up fleeing the law for the better part of a year. In this time he traveled thousands of miles evading arrest despite nationwide warrants and exposure on 'Unsolved Mysteries.' In May '97 Gary turned himself in and was eventually convicted of homicide. After serving time in Texas prison he was released and deported from the United States. Today he lives with his wife and children in Calgary where he is a business owner.

Where Then O Bliss (Excerpt)

Part One

Chapter 1

Where then, O bliss, is thy balm?
Where, O rapture, thine infinite?

Allen Bill Pond...

As the sun lies dying at Allen Bill Pond, thoughts of Felicia fill the recess of my mind.

Felicia of the unpronounceable last name. Felicia, Felicia, Felicia...

Actually, her name is Felicja, but it corresponds to Felicia in English. Fay-lee-tsya in her native Poland, Fe-lee-sha over here.

I met Felicia early last year. We were both enrolled in an intensive course of environmental studies. Though we were part of a small group of twenty or so people attending long classes daily, we are both standoffish enough that it took us a few days to introduce ourselves to each other and become acquainted. By the time we did do so, it had already become as clear to her as it was to me that we were kindred spirits.

What is it that identifies a kindred spirit, Reader? As I sit here twirling my pen pondering this, the main thing that seems to stand out is intelligence — intelligence as seen in the eyes and the poise or bearing of a person, intelligence plus a little je ne sais quoi. At least, that's what comes to mind as I think of this in relation to Felicia. I don't recall any specific action or words on her part that revealed her to me any more clearly than did the intelligence and that special something I could see in her eyes and poise. I like to think too that the same applied in regard to her perception of me, but be that as it may. What I do know is that when Felicia saw me spending my time staring out the window rather than paying attention in class, she figured that she had found a kindred spirit; and when she heard me introduce myself to the class by saying my name, pausing, wrinkling my brow and then slowly continuing with, "I can think of all kinds of things about myself that I don't want to tell you, but I'm having trouble coming up with anything I do want to tell you," she knew that she'd found one.

Felicia is beautiful. This is true and necessary, necessary twice over. First, this is a story I'm writing. Never mind the fact that it might be perceived by some as a true story. It is still a story, and in our culture the female lead in a story, be it a book, movie or whatever else, is beautiful. It's one of the failings of our culture. And secondly, I myself incarnate this same weakness such that I'm able to love only beautiful women. Try as I might, and believe me I have tried hard, I am completely unable to arouse any passion within myself for the plain-Janes of this world, no matter that they are often the more beautiful in spirit.

That said, let me tell you, Reader, how beautiful Felicia is. She once told me that Polish girls in general are beautiful. I believe her. I have no reason to disbelieve her. Felicia is slender and of medium height. I never saw her with dark hair, even though that's her natural color. Always when I knew her she was blonde, sometimes a straw-blonde and sometimes with a hint of henna. The color of one's hair by no means determines or even enhances beauty, but when Felicia's visiting mother-in-law was pressuring her to go back to brunette, I thwarted the matron's efforts with a single disparaging remark — merely because I did not want my beautiful girl to change in any way.

Felicia's eyes are the color of the Seine, a soft and serene brown lightened with flecks of green. I've enjoyed many, many hours diving into those waters, basking in the subtlety of the main current, being tickled by the tug of innumerable undercurrents. I dare say no more — dare think no more — of Felicia's eyes.

Although a picture says a thousand words, the reverse is not true: A thousand words do not say a picture. This is a pity because it makes it difficult for me to help you envision Felicia. When she was without a speck of make-up, I found her beautiful in a very Slavic way. I would mention full lips, wide spacing of eyes and prominent cheekbones, for whatever illumination that might cast. Made up, she looks very Euro, very enchantress-mystery-of-kohl; she is the fin-de-siècle answer to, image of, Brigitte Bardot.

Is Felicia a smiler, a sunny personality? Need you ask, Reader?

I knew Felicia to smile but seldom. Her smiles were like gems, rare and precious. I think — rather, I should say that I know —

that this was something that drew her to me. I am confused within myself as to what I mean by this: On the one hand, it is true that she perceived me, as it seems does everyone, to be as austere in countenance as I have just described her. She once saw some old photos of me in which I had long blond hair and I was just staring existentially at the camera. She was struck by these photos. She saw herself in them. And she was right. It might as well have been her staring at the camera, thinly disguised, very thinly disguised, by my features. But on the other hand, appearances can be, and in this case are, deceiving, for I am a veritable well of optimism and inner sanguinity. Unlike Felicia, whose solemnity of demeanor is due to a profound sadness, my own is more akin to ennui. So I'm not entirely unconfused as to whether she was drawn to a bird of her own feather, or attracted to an opposite. I suspect that, paradoxically, both are true.

Let me get Jean-Paul and France out of the way right now. No conscious attempt has been made to season the preceding passages along such lines. The simple fact is that Felicia is a true Pole and the heart of every true Pole lives in Paris no matter whether the body resides there too or in Chicago, London or Warsaw itself. For me to think or talk about Felicia completely without reference to things French would be both nonsensical and impossible; it would be like talking about Catherine the Great with no mention of Russia, Cleopatra without Rome,

Helen sans Troy — simply preposterous.

Have I given you a fair enough picture of Felicia yet? Are you able to visualize an image that is more personality than anonymity? Can you begin to comprehend her beauty? Now let me tell you the anomaly: Felicia wears glasses. We all know from Hollywood's teaching that a beautiful girl need do nothing more strenuous than donning a pair of glasses to turn herself into a frump, a wallflower ignored by all men. (Didn't Marilyn Monroe, of all people, do this precise thing in one or more of her movies?) And of course we also know what baloney that is, for various reasons. Well, interestingly enough, in Felicia's case this "wallflower effect" is very nearly fully realized. This is because of her lens prescription. When nearsighted people wear glasses, others do not see their eyes to appear magnified; in fact, the opposite is true, but it is only with strong lenses that the eyes appear noticeably shrunken. It is farsighted people who wear glasses that make their eyes appear magnified ("googly-eyed", to use the scientific term); but since most farsighted people wear glasses only while reading (or not at all, for that matter), it's really a small percentage of regular glasses-wearers whose appearance is actually changed very drastically by the donning of glasses. It just so happens, though, that Felicia is one of these. She is farsighted, and worse yet (in this respect), farsighted in only one eye. When she was a child growing up in Poland, she had a severe bout with one of the childhood diseases. Due to the lack there at the time of the appropriate medication, she almost lost her young life, but ended up pulling through. This affliction left its mark on her, though, in the form of a scarred retina in one eye. Imagine, then, our Felicia having just put on her glasses as described. It really does not matter, does it, how beautiful she is? She has effectively concealed her beauty and transformed herself into the proverbial wallflower.

***End of excerpt from* Where Then O Bliss.**

THE AGE OF SOPHISTRY (an essay excerpted from **Bioism: The Deity of** ***Life)***

Though all are born philosophers, few remain so. Philosophy, Philosophy, wherefore art thou, Philosophy?

Is it me? – my imagination? Am I jaded? Or is there a dearth of philosophy today? Knowledge, good knowledge, real knowledge, certainly is not lacking. Nor is the love of it. Philognosy – if I may invent a word – is alive and kicking. We are swimming in a vast ocean of knowledge, perhaps even drowning in knowledge. Yet, where is wisdom? Knowledge, knowledge, everywhere; but where is wisdom? Where is philosophy?

After two and a half millennia of philosophy, the greatest philosopher of all remains Socrates, the progenitor of the breed, a stonemason who penned not a single word for posterity. Who is there nowadays that compares to him? Nobody. Nobody! Him, one simple stonemason, versus us in our sophistication and our billions, scientists, engineers, doctors, mathematicians, theologians, not to mention stonemasons and carpenters too. All we seem to manage, all I seem to see in looking around, is sophistry, a uniform horizon of sophistry.

The problem with philosophy in the modern age is not with the state of human knowledge, nor with that of human intelligence – both of which are more advanced now than ever before, nor even with that of human virtue, the disappearance or degradation of which is mourned anew unceasingly by each succeeding generation. No, the problem with philosophy today stems from none of these things. The problem with philosophy stems from the vastness of the field human knowledge has revealed to us. The philosopher, the true philosopher, is a general who must survey this whole field; he is an Alexander who must acquaint himself with his theatre of war in its entirety. The problem with philosophy today is that whereas we need generals, we have only champions; whereas we need strategy, we are offered only tactics; whereas we need an Arthur, we are given instead a brigade, a division, an army, of Lancelots. The problem with philosophy today is with the philosophers of today, men blinded to the forest by the trees, daunted by the vastness of the field, drowning in the ocean where they swim. The problem with philosophy today is that the generalists have surrendered to the specialists.

Is it any wonder that superstition is once again rearing its ugly head? – that this Hydra is rearing its multitude of heads, old and new? Don't blame the specialists – the physicists with their wave-particles, the astronomers with their multiverses, the psychologists with their envies, to name but a few – who view reality through the narrow lenses of their own disciplines. A gravitation toward the outré is all too easy (too pride-reassuring, really) whenever expert knowledge reaches a plateau in comprehension, an obstacle to progress, a moment of inadequacy. Don't blame the specialists! Blame the generalists! Blame the philosophers! Blame philosophy! For philosophy is our bulwark against superstition, against both superstition and the sophistry that feeds and nourishes it.

***End of essay excerpted from* Bioism: The Deity of Life.**

www.ingramcontent.com/pod-product-compliance
Lightning Source LLC
Chambersburg PA
CBHW022207050726
47590CB00002B/678

* 9 7 8 0 9 7 8 4 9 9 2 6 6 *